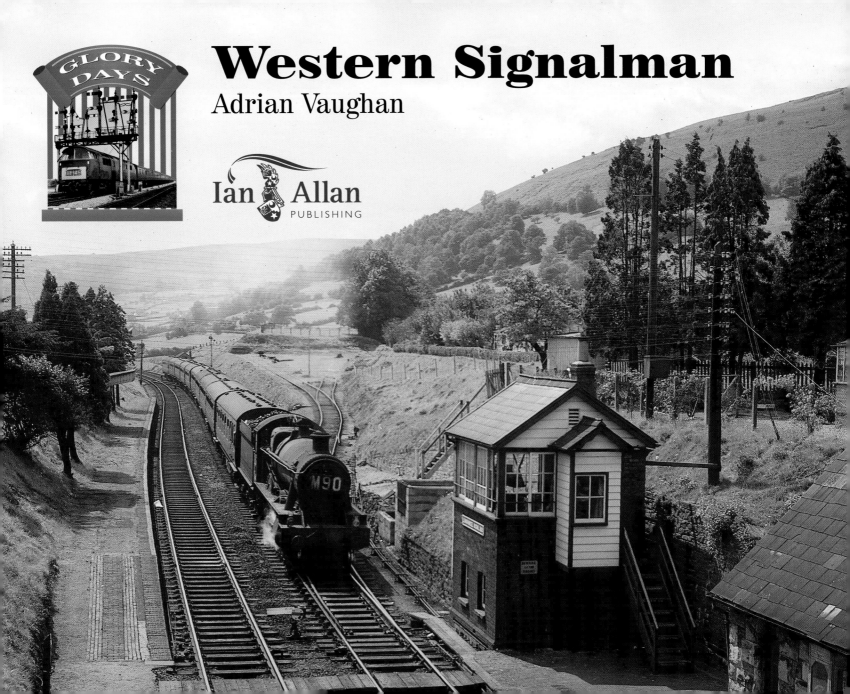

GLORY DAYS

Western Signalman

Adrian Vaughan

Ian Allan
PUBLISHING

First published 2000

ISBN 0 7110 2715 3

Published by Ian Allan Publishing

an imprint of Ian Allan Publishing Ltd, Terminal House, Shepperton, Surrey TW17 8AS.

Printed by Ian Allan Printing Ltd, Riverdene Business Park, Hersham, Surrey KT12 4RG.

Code: 0005/B2

Dedication

For Larry,

Western signalman

Contents

Acknowledgements

I am pleased to acknowledge the assistance I received from the experts of the Signalling Record Society in interpreting the photographs: Mike Christensen, Larry Crosier, Reg Instone, Peter Jordan, Peter Kay, John Morris, David Collins and Garth Tilt. I would also like to thank the photographers, for their co-operation in 1999 and for their patience 40 years ago in waiting for hours by the line to get their pictures: David Anderson, Hugh Ballantyne, Mike Esau, Pat Garland, Peter Gray, K. R. Pirt, R. C. Riley and also Ron White of Colour-Rail.

Anyone wishing to know more about railway signalling should apply to the Signalling Record Society, Membership Secretary, Barry Bridges, 44 Founceley Avenue, Dane End, Ware, Herts SG12 0NQ.

Introduction

The Great Western Railway did not die in 1948. Only the title changed. The men who arrived for work in the signalboxes on 1 January 1948 were the ones who had signed off duty the night before.

The GWR directors had long considered the railway to be a very great, public service institution and this fitted in well with the feelings of their men. Nationalisation strengthened that feeling because, as old-hand railwaymen (and indeed, even my grandfather — who had always been a lorry driver) said, 'They're *our* railways now.' Of course there were millions who disagreed with nationalisation in 1948 but not very many of these were railwaymen. It is true that a handful of Traffic Department supervisory staff at Divisional level, those completely unable to accept the politics of nationalisation, resigned and went to work on the railways of the British Empire. And this was strange because these railways had always been state-owned. Perhaps there was something in the colonial situation which was more congenial to them than the new democracy of Britain.

The railwaymen and women of 1948 were very experienced people in their work; one could say they were 'battle-hardened' — either by wartime air raids and hard work on short rations, or from actual battle. These people did their work with a sense of responsibility, of personal pride — and with minimal supervision. There were of course small mishaps but such incidents were dealt with expertly and — with plenty of experienced men on hand and with the organisation under one control — quickly. I know that my feelings, and those of the enthusiastic railwaymen I knew, were not universal, and for the opposite view my readers should consult *The Railway Workers* by Frank McKenna.

This book is designed in two parts to show the double-sided attraction of the railway. With the pictures I hope to show the physical attractions of the railway, the handsomeness which is pleasing to humanity. With words, I hope to illustrate the spirit of the mechanical railway. Operating difficulties and physical hardships were interesting challenges and were a form of permanent outward-bound course — in a mild form — which drew people together into a team to serve the public. It was not an *ersatz* team spirit imposed from above, out of some 'Plan' purchased from an American company of consultants, but a real team spirit which arose organically out of friendships in long service together. People knew each other of old, they shared hardships — three or four signalmen who spent more than one soaking wet weekend together as handsignalmen or platelayers constantly out in all weathers — and consequently there was respect between them. Sometimes in a permanent-way gang there were two or more members of the same family. Long service created folklore, the legends of the great deeds and the daft ones which, like a regimental history, made a fertile soil from which the team spirit grew.

Even the automated railway needs a few people to operate the computers. Dedication is always required but it is more difficult to be dedicated to a keyboard than to a signalbox full of polished steel and brass with a train of passengers outside that you can see. The mechanical railway required the best human sentiments and emotions in order for it to work well. Steam engines were at the heart of it — the grandeur of the locomotive was vital — but they were still only a part. They would not have worked without the courage of their crews. Every reasonable human being will rise to meet a challenge and is a better person for having done so.

Automation was inevitable but it destroyed a way of life. It has been bad for people because their humanity has been diminished, their stress has increased and job prospects shortened. It is not surprising that those of us who knew the old railway, and its people, look back on it with affection.

My friend Larry Crosier started on the Great Western Railway in 1943 and rose to be a Special Class Signalman in Laira Junction box. Larry is typical of the majority of signalmen I met in his commitment to the job but, luckily for us, he is unusual in that he retains a photographic memory of his career. A shortened biography of his working life shows perfectly the humanity and the informality of the mechanical railway.

No 4911 *Bowden Hall* was fatally wounded by a German bomb at Keyham on 30 April 1941. The engine took the blast, saved the houses from demolition and probably saved the life of the Keyham signalbox. The engine was subsequently scrapped.
Larry Crosier Collection

Bickleigh signalbox interior in 1957, looking towards Yelverton, showing the GWR 1890-pattern 'twist locking' frame; note the unusually broad, highly-polished, cast iron treads between the levers. Above these, a lightly-loaded instrument shelf carries the keyless bells rung by Yelverton and Marsh Mills; the Bickleigh signalman transmits his bell codes to those places on the plunger of the electric train token instrument. On the right is the instrument allowing the signalman to release the ganger's occupation key while locking the electric train token instruments, thus making it safe for the ganger to place a trolley on the single line. The signalman has protected his highly polished floor with cardboard.
Larry Crosier

St Blazey Bridge · St Blazey · St Austell · Par · Treverrin · Lostwithiel · Onslow Sidings · A · Bodmin Road · Largin

Par Bridge · Pinnock Tunnel · Par Harbour

Doublebois · Menheniot · Trerule · St Germans · Wearde · Saltash · Royal Albert Bridge · Devonport · Devonport Jc · Plymouth North Road West · B
A · Liskeard · Coombe Jc · St Budeaux West* · St Budeaux East* · Keyham · Cornwall Jc · Millbay Stn. · Millbay Crossing
Looe

Plymouth North Road East · Yelverton · Bickleigh · Marsh Mills* · Laira Jc · Hemerdon · Ivybridge* · Brent* · Tigley
B · Mannamead · Lipson Jc* · Tavistock Jc (Telegraphist) · Plympton* · Cornwood* · Wrangaton* · Rattery*
Mount Gould Jc

*Signalboxes at which Larry Crosier did not work.

4

Porter at Bickleigh

Larry was born in St Budeaux, Plymouth, on 31 March 1929. The railways of that area were handsome and complex, with both GWR and SR signals, locomotives, carriages and architecture. Larry grew up a keen train and signal spotter. He was by no means the only dedicated railwayman whose loyalty has been nurtured from an early age through the encouragement of friendly railwaymen.

He was 11½ when World War 2 broke out and, as he lived not far from the docks, had first-hand experience of some severe bombing. On the evening of 30 April 1941, Larry was under attack — along with the rest of Plymouth — from high-explosive and incendiary bombs. Not far away from his home that evening, No 4911 *Bowden Hall*, hauling the 3.30pm Paddington-Penzance express, was brought to a standstill at Keyham station under air-raid 'red' regulations because of the blitz. A bomb fell on the track close to the engine, which was fatally damaged, but in taking the blast it saved the houses and their occupants from serious injury. The signalman at Keyham box that day was Charlie Austin. When Larry was a lad telegraphist at Tavistock Junction box in 1946 he used to walk home with Charlie at the end of each shift and on one of these occasions Charlie told Larry how, on that particular evening in 1941 when the 'Red' alert sounded, he had entered his corrugated iron shelter within the signalbox and shortly afterwards had heard a fearsome explosion followed by a series of terrific blows on his shelter which crushed it and almost him within it. During the air raids on Plymouth scores of thousands of these white phosphorous fire bombs were dropped — frequently on the railway. Signalmen would sally forth from their shelters to cover the phosphorous with sand to extinguish the bombs.

Not even Hitler's Luftwaffe could prevent Larry from enjoying the signalboxes and steam locomotives. By the time he was 14 he was well practised in the working of the 36-lever St Budeaux East signalbox and was learning the 60-lever Plymouth North Road West. This became possible because one of the lad telegraphists — or booking boys — for North Road West lived near Larry and was a friend, and the signalmen for this box, Cecil Wilcox, also lived in St Budeaux. When Cecil was on 12-hour Sunday day turn, Mrs Wilcox would send him his Sunday roast — all the more precious in those days of rationing — by train. She put the meal between two plates wrapped around with a couple of towels and sent it to her husband by taking it to St Budeaux station and handing it to the guard of the 1.40pm Saltash to Plymouth railcar. The West box booking boy went to the station to meet the train and it was he who suggested that Larry should meet the train and take the meal to the box. Thus he got into North Road West around midday and left on the 5.55 out to St Budeaux.

Larry understood how to keep a simple train register and now the North Road West booking boy coached him in the far more complicated job of keeping the record for this very busy box. This of course was in the time before biro pens, when the pen was a simple steel nib with a wooden handle and the ink mixed up from powder. Once Larry was competent he could perform the occasional, unofficial, relief for his booking boy mate if there was a particular film he wished to see or — once every couple of months — when he went round all the boxes in the area collecting 'slate club' money.

The mechanical action of the signalling rarely failed but signal wires broke occasionally. Larry was with Cecil Wilcox in North Road West one evening. An up Southern train was waiting to leave Platform 2. Larry obtained 'Line Clear' from Devonport Junction with the bell code for a Southern Railway stopping train: 2-2-1-3. Cecil set the points out of the platform but the wire to the No 3 signal, exiting from the platform, broke as he pulled the lever. Without hesitation, Cecil picked up an emergency 'sling' for reconnecting the severed wire, said, 'Look after the box, boy,' to Larry and hurried off to follow the wire-run and find the fault. It was nowhere to be seen and must therefore be beneath the wooden platform. Cecil went to the driver of the train, authorised him to pass the platform signal at danger and, when the train had gone, crawled under the platform, bound the broken ends of the wire around the 'eyes' of the sling and everything was back to normal again until the Signal & Telegraph lineman could come to make a permanent repair. Delay negligible.

Larry tried for a job on the GWR when he left school in December 1942 but there were no vacancies, so he got a job in the Co-op bakery and went to the Chief Inspector's Millbay offices each Saturday morning to inquire for a vacancy. From there he would go to St Budeaux or North Road West or North Road East, depending on who was on duty. North Road East box was run by two signalmen whom Larry described as 'a great old pair of characters', Bert and 'Huddy' — Sid Huddison. There was little chance of being caught in the box by the District Inspector on a Saturday and no-one ever thought that the stationmaster of this busy place would think of calling in on a Saturday when the station was at its busiest. One Saturday morning who should they see walking off the end of Platform 7 towards the box but the stationmaster. Larry felt very awkward and said he would leave at once but Bert would not hear of it. He was a firm believer in encouraging willing young signalmen of the future. Up the stairs came the station boss. He saw Larry standing there — and presumably looking very guilty — and called Bert to the top of the stairs. Clearly he was remonstrating with him for allowing a trespasser in the box but Bert was having none of it. He had a habit of emphasising a point by cupping one hand and bringing the edge of the other hand down sharply into it. Bert told the stationmaster that Larry was applying every Saturday for a job on the railway and that he was a signalman of the future. The stationmaster decided that Bert knew what he was doing, that discretion was the better part of valour, and left the box.

There was no 'booking' to do in the East box, unless there was an emergency to record, and after several Saturday shifts Larry had learned the frame quite well. Bert obviously thought so, for one Saturday he asked Larry to take over his end of the frame for half an hour because he wanted to go and get his hair cut. Larry was only too pleased. This was about 10am. Bert did not come back until 12.30 and was met by a very irate Huddy. 'If you can bugger off, so can I!' he snapped, and picking up his hat and coat, stomped off down the stairs. So Larry then worked the west end of the frame until 2pm. (In my own experience, in 1965, Peter, the 16-year-old booking boy at Hampton Court Junction — admittedly with only about 42 levers but with trains from several directions passing about once a minute — kept the Train Register up to date *and* worked the box entirely unassisted.)

Larry's persistence was finally rewarded when, on 4 October 1943, he started as a lad porter at Yelverton, junction for Princetown, earning £1 7s 3d (£1.36) a week. All railway workers travelling by rail to work paid for their ticket and Larry's six-monthly season ticket from Plymouth cost £1 16s. The stationmaster at Yelverton was Mr Badcock. Under him at the station were the signalmen, Mr Willmott and Fred Nicholas, his son Jimmy Thomas was porter, his son Eric was porter-signalman and Ken Gay was the other lad porter. Ken was to become the last guard of the Princetown branch train.

Ken, being senior to Larry, divided their duties to his liking but Larry was so keen he did not mind having all the most difficult jobs. A very nice job which, the hierarchy being what it was, devolved to Larry, was to clean the signalbox handlamp. Larry did this on his first day, the first time he had ever had a legitimate excuse for visiting a signalbox. He found the signalbox interior very strange after the big, main-line boxes. The greatest difference was that because it was a single-line box, there was no instrument shelf over the levers. The very large and cumbersome electric train staff signalling instruments stood at the back of the box.

The signalman asked Larry his name and Larry told him. 'Well,' said the signalman, 'my name is *Mister* Willmott with two 'l's and two 't's. Larry never addressed him as anything other than 'Mister Willmott' afterwards. 'What are you doing on the railway?' asked Mr Willmott.

'I want to be a signalman.'

'Oh — and what's your father do?'

'He's in the Navy, Mr Willmott. He served his time and came out but now he's been called back in.'

'Do you think he could get me a pair of Navy boots?'. Larry said he'd see and later was able to present Mr Willmott with his heart's desire. After that he was well in and Mr Willmott told him to be sure to come to the signalbox at meal times to warm his food in the oven of the signalbox stove. He also gave him a copy of the Red Book — the 1936 *GWR Regulations for Train Signalling on Double and Single Lines*.

There was no piped drinking water at Yelverton, so water for the signalbox was collected and stored in a pair of 2-gallon cans, one in use at the box, the other standing on the ground near the tunnel mouth, filling up from a trickle of water which ran down the rock face of the cutting. At intervals, the purity of the water was tested by the railway chemist at Swindon — but a sample was not sent to Swindon by train, oh no! The chemist used to come down to delightful Yelverton from Swindon to collect the sample himself. The lavatory cisterns were filled with water from the moorland stream that supplied the locomotive water tank. Larry washed the floor of the Yelverton lavatories with cold water and Jeyes Fluid, and the signal lamps he burnished as the stationmaster required — with Bath brick and paraffin. The wicks were cut off sharply horizontal, the burner polished, the vessel filled with paraffin and wiped dry of any spillage. Not only were the lamps inspected by Mr Badcock and Ken Gay but there was also a Plymouth Divisional Lamp Inspector, Mr Reeby, who was responsible for all signal lamps from Totnes to Penzance and the branches. The GWR believed it employed no more people than it had to but even so the company's idea of 'the bare essentials' seems lavish by today's standards. The railway worked properly because it was well staffed with conscientious people.

Ken Gay took Larry to the relatively short signal post at the platform end and showed him how to open the lamp case and place the cleaned lamp within. He then told him that, as junior man, he would now have to change the lamps in the up and down main distant signals and also the up branch distant and down advanced starting signal on the branch. Larry asked how he was to get to the up main distant, since there was a tunnel just off the end of the platform. 'Well,' said Ken, 'by rights you're supposed to walk round by road but it's a long way and the distant's not far beyond the Tavistock end of the tunnel, so we go through the tunnel when the boss goes for his dinner.' Larry walked through the tunnel, to the up distant signal which was a little way beyond the tunnel portal. He climbed the 30ft ladder and replaced the old with the newly-serviced lamp just as a Plymouth-bound passenger train passed. He then followed it into the tunnel, carrying the old lamp. The tunnel was 641yd long and he was soon blinded by the smoke still hanging in the air. He did not think of turning back — he had a job to do — but instead stood in a safety recess in the tunnel wall until the air cleared. This took some time and as he set off again he saw, out in the daylight at the station, a '64xx' class pannier tank leaving the station towards the tunnel with a train of empty cattle trucks for Coryton. The engine's whistle echoed deafeningly as the train entered the tunnel. He pressed himself against the sooty wall as the train stormed past. In pitch darkness there was only smoke, orange firelight, fumes, echoing exhaust and clattering cattle trucks.

Larry's GWR uniform arrived at the station after he had been there for a couple of weeks. It came with a gas mask and a military steel helmet. He took the brown paper parcel, chrysalis-like, into the gents' toilet and emerged, five minutes later, changed into a brass-buttoned GWR employee.

Yelverton was at the summit of a 1 in 60 climb from the north, Tavistock, and the south, Marsh Mills. There was a Stop Board at each end of the station, at which freight trains stopped to pin down wagon handbrakes. Being also the junction for the Princetown line, there was a lot of train activity there and it was indeed generally a very handsome country station.

The Princetown branch platform and the up platform to Plymouth formed one 'V'-shaped block on which stood the main station buildings, with the down platform 'staggered', the signalbox at the Plymouth end. Because the platforms were not opposite each other, it was not possible to use a trolley or four-wheel barrow to carry parcels from one platform to the other. Parcels traffic arrived from Plymouth and was considerable. Princetown parcels were left on the down platform and the early morning train from Princetown would run off the branch, along the up direction crossing loop and into the tunnel until the rear vehicle was clear of the points to the down loop, and then set back into the down platform to load Princetown traffic, then return to the branch where more shunting, of an unusual kind, was necessary to put the engine at the Princetown end of the train. The 8.36am and 2.50pm Yelverton-Princetown trains ran 'mixed'. That is to say they had a passenger coach (brake composite) next to the engine, usually a '4402' 2-6-2 tank, and behind the coach, freight wagons and a freight brake van. Any goods traffic from the previous day was left in Yelverton down refuge siding for the 8.36am to Princetown, while the 7.50am Laira-Horrabridge goods also carried Princetown traffic. The 12.14pm Princetown would run through to Horrabridge to pick up this traffic and work it back to Princetown as the 2.50pm mixed.

The Princetown train was guarded, in this era, by Frank Prowse, whose 'GWR' lapel roundels were embroidered in goods guard red, not passenger guard yellow. His brake van — branded 'PRINCETOWN R.U. NOT IN COMMON USE' — did not normally leave the branch and was practically his private property. He had it fitted out with curtains at the window and polished lino on the floor. Yelverton's track layout provided a crossing loop on the main line but only a single track and turntable siding on the branch. To run the engine round its train for the journey back to Princetown, the engine pushed the coach and brake van towards Princetown until they were beyond the points to the siding. Frank screwed his handbrake on, the engine was uncoupled, ran forward and set back into the turntable siding. Now letting off his handbrake, Frank allowed the short train to roll back to the platform. The engine could follow when it had turned.

From time to time the Princetown train arrived with the brake van part of the coach piled with mail bags sewn by the convicts. These had then to be loaded on to a four-wheel barrow and hauled round to the up platform, ready to be manhandled into a Plymouth-bound passenger train. In Larry's time the Launceston/Tavistock guards would not allow time to be lost for any cause and certainly not for loading convict mail bags. On the day that Larry's nice new uniform arrived, the 6pm Princetown-Tavistock arrived at Yelverton with a load of mail bags at 6.38. The 6.30 Tavistock arrived at 6.45, scheduled to cross the 6.10 Plymouth-Launceston. This was wartime and all work outside after sunset was carried out in darkness. The trains ran with their blinds drawn. Larry and

his mates loaded all the mail bags the Tavistock guard would allow and the rest would have to wait for a later train. When Larry went off duty and got off the pitch dark platform into the brightly lit interior of the compartment, he saw for the first time the filthy state of his uniform, smothered in dust and thousands of pieces of flock from the mail bags.

Larry's work also involved loading carts into ASMO and MOGO vans. These were purpose-built for vehicles and had end loading doors. The wagons were placed buffer to buffer and the carts pushed right through to the far end. (A slightly less effective way of loading is used today in the Channel Tunnel Shuttle trains.) His work also took him to Clearbrook Halt, where a woman porter covered 7am to 4pm and Ken Gay or Larry covered until 6.50pm. This too is an improvement on the present-day practice of having entirely unmanned stations, never mind *halts*.

Larry was transferred to the yard master's office at Tavistock Junction yard

in December 1943. He began at 8am one Monday morning as telegraph boy. He travelled on the 7.10am North Road to Marsh Mills and walked back to the signalbox from there — the train he had just vacated snorting away uphill, through the semi-darkness, into the country. His path took him by Tavistock Junction signalbox. The lights were on, shining out into the freezing gloom, and as he walked past Larry could see the promise of gleaming lever tops and the backs of the many instruments, and longed to go up there and see in full the polished interior.

The Tavistock Junction Yard Inspector was Bert Hunt, who had risen to command the complex marshalling yard from the rank of shunter. His schooling would have been minimal but his railway experience and his native intelligence were clearly very great. He was a modest man with a good humour and used to boast that, in his young days as a shunter, he had been known as 'Whippet Quick', because he was the fastest runner in the yard in pursuit of

Bickleigh station, looking towards Tavistock on 15 July 1961, with No 5572 on a Plymouth-Tavistock waiting for an up train to arrive. Note the full '6ft' space between the tracks, a reminder that this was once 7ft gauge track. The house on the rise belonged in 1950 to Col Johnson, whose business was Chinese geese which came to him in crates by passenger train.
R. C. Riley

On 1 August 1959, with No 6830 *Buckenhill Grange* standing opposite the 153-lever Newton Abbot West signalbox on the down relief line, a double-headed express, reporting number 425, goes by nonstop on the down through line and joins the down relief. It is piloted by a 'Castle', with train engine No 6002 *King William IV*. The left-hand pair in the group of four signals apply to the down relief line platform, starting along the relief line or onto the down main. The right-hand pair apply to the down main line face of that platform, starting along the down main or to the down relief line.
Peter W. Gray

wagons but now, as Yard Inspector, he suffered from rheumatism and was known as 'Hopalong Cassidy'. Larry worked in a low-ceilinged room 10ft by 8ft. Its door from the yard was protected by a concrete anti-bomb blast wall about 3ft from the door and the windows were practically blocked by blast walls 2ft from the glass. Its grim interior was illuminated by a single, central, electric bulb. Beneath this was a chair at a table which carried two dialling phones, while around the walls were 10 wooden-cased 'bus-line' telephones and the much larger wooden cabinet of the phone to the control office.

The arrangement of telephone circuits was typically railway — piecemeal. There were some direct lines, such as those that could be dialled or to the controllers. Signalboxes and stations within a short range could be contacted on the 'bus line' phone by turning the central knob to the designated number and then pressing the button below the correct number of times. With messages for places beyond the Plymouth District, Larry called Millbay telegraph office.

Before each freshly marshalled freight train left the yard, its guard came to Larry with complete details and it was his job to compose the message in the correct style and forward it to all those departments which needed to have the information. He phoned the exchange with a message something like this:

'Tavi Junc to SM [stationmaster], Loco Newton Abbot; SM, Loco Control Exeter; Loco Taunton, YM [yard master] Bristol West Depot; Control Bristol and Mr Coulam, Bristol.

'11.40pm Truro to Banbury. Time. [Departed right time] Flanders [trainmen's home depot]. Laira. Cole, [this was the actual name of the guard] Tavi Junc.' [The names of the enginemen were never given but that of the guard was.] 'Bunker [Loco class and home depot] 2831. Laira.

'10 Woodford, 5 Sheffield, 7 Banbury, 8 Oxford, 5 Leamington, 10 Bristol West Depot, 5 Swindon.'

A heavy train like this would require banking assistance and Larry would advise the Totnes signalman to have the banker standing by with the message: 'Prune 11.40 Truro. Time.'

Every train had to be fully 'wired on'. The Millbay transfer trips or the Laira-Tavistock Junction, or the Truro pick-up goods. The latter, by the way, was so slow, because of all the shunting at each wayside station in wartime, that it was known as 'The Snaily', took eight or 10 hours for the 57 miles and was thus a 'double home' or 'lodging turn' for the train crew — down to Truro one day, back the next. Besides 'wiring' all the outward trains, Larry took all the incoming train information from Control and then passed the information on to his inspector and any other interested party. The Tavistock Junction Yard number-takers were not train spotters but railway staff whose job it was to keep close account of every wagon standing in the yard; all the comings and goings. At the commencement of each shift they brought into Larry's office the wagon-by-wagon account — or 'stour' — of the entire contents of the yard: empty wagons, loaded, with what and where to. This information had to be wired on to Control so that arrangements could be made for working the traffic and for putting on extra trains if necessary. Larry was 15 years old carrying this responsibility and the commitment to punctual attendance, promptitude and accuracy.

When he was on late turn, finishing at 10pm, there was a mad rush through the yard to catch the last bus, which dropped him at Milehouse bus depot, leaving him a 1½-mile walk home. Sometimes, walking home so late, the air raid sirens sounded and he would take shelter in any house he was passing. Once he knocked on the front door and a huge woman opened it, threw her arms round him and dragged him inside crying, 'Oh — look at the poor little chap!' Larry must have been a lot slimmer then than now! Outside the ack-ack guns made a terrific racket while their shrapnel showered back — breaking roofs and bouncing on pavements while the bombs fell and burst.

Larry was soon asked to learn the booking lad's job in Tavistock Junction signalbox. His reputation as an amateur booking boy seemed not to have reached Tavi Yard and he never admitted to knowing 75% of the job already. He soon familiarised himself with the other 25% — the details of bells and working that existed in that particular box — and was given 10 out of 10 for quickness. He was appointed relief booking lad for the box and continued also as telegraph boy in the yard office. By June 1944 he was the permanent booking lad there.

In many signalboxes the windows were completely covered over with black paper on portable frames but with just one pane at each end left clear so that the signalmen could see the tail lamps of trains. But this was not the case at Tavistock Junction. At this box the lampshades were the size and shape of half a football and were fitted reversed, bowl uppermost, to deflect the light from the electric bulb upwards on to the ceiling. The light was subdued and the bowls became filled with dead flies.

Tavistock Junction box was in direct contact with Air Raid Control, which telephoned the messages: 'Air Raid Yellow', 'Air Raid Purple' and 'Air Raid Red' to the booking boy. At 'Air Raid Red' all work ceased as Larry operated the master switch in the box which doused all the lights in the yard. During a red alert on 29 April 1941 the 3.30pm Paddington-Penzance had stopped at Keyham and the engine, No 4911 *Bowden Hall*, was wrecked by a bomb falling by the cab. (See picture.)

Tavistock Junction box had 105 levers: 1 to 56 for the down road, 61 to 105 for the up. Lever 85 worked a set of points operated by electric motors. They had been installed in 1943 and were always giving trouble with 'detection', because the ground was soft and sinking. When they went wrong, sometimes in the middle of the night, and if Larry was on duty, it was his job to go and fetch the lineman from his home in Plympton. Larry recalls the points failing when an 'Air Raid Purple' warning was on and walking to Plympton, through Tavi Yard, up on to the road and out into open country and, hearing the guns start up, turning to look back towards Plymouth to see the flashes of guns and bombs and hear the accompanying racket.

Larry left Tavistock Junction box early in 1948 to work as a shunter in the yard. In May he was conscripted into the Devonshire Regiment but was soon transferred to the Railway Operating Division of the Royal Engineers. He was discharged from his National Service in 1949, aged 20. He was disciplined, self-reliant, well trained — and just longing to get back to work on his beloved railway. He left the Army on a month's leave, but at once went along to the District Inspector at North Road, Percy May, to find out the job which had been allocated to him as a returning soldier, and was sent to be the porter-signalman at Bickleigh. He was back on the Tavistock branch the following Monday.

There were two shifts at Bickleigh. On weekdays early turn covered 6am to 2.20pm and late turn from 12.20 to 10.10pm. Larry worked as a signalman from 12.35 to 2.10pm. On Saturdays the full shifts were 7.40am-4pm and 3.50pm-11.10pm with three hours in the box. Had he been working anywhere on the main line, he would have been paid for an 88-hour fortnight and the rest would have been overtime but on the Tavistock branch they were still working a 48-hour, six-day week before getting overtime. Larry cared little for these payroll matters. He was getting paid to work in a lovely spot with enough to do to keep him busy. Half of his time had to be spent attending to passengers at Shaugh Bridge platform, including Sundays when a great many day trippers came out there to climb the rocks and walk in the woods beside the tumbling river. The traffic at Bickleigh included bees — charged as for 'company's risk' but sent at 'owner's risk' — loaded horseboxes on Wednesdays during the summer stud season and troops to and from the Royal Marines' camp just outside Bickleigh village.

When the regiment went on leave, 500 names and destinations, on one large warrant, were brought to the station and Larry and the signalman had the job of writing out 500 individual paper tickets. They wrote in indelible pencil and put double-sided carbon paper between the ticket and the counterfoil, so that the ticket could not be altered and soldierly fiddles were prevented.

Long shadows on a perfect summer evening. No 6956 on the 7.14pm Exeter stopping train passing Hackney Yard (Newton Abbot) down inner home signals. *Peter W. Gray*

A quiet Sunday, waiting a while between trains but No 6029 was worth waiting for on the 1.20pm Paddington-Penzance express on 13 May 1956. Sunday peace was shattered by the gunfire of *King Edward VIII* taking 15 coaches — 500 tons — past Hackney Yard. The signal arms read from left to right: down main to yard reception line 2; to reception 1; to down goods loop; down main inner home; with Newton Abbot East's distant below. This distant signal could only be cleared when the road at Newton East was set for the down through line. The 'Cornish Riviera' was routed through Newton Abbot on the down main and so this distant signal was, in theory, the first that the driver would meet, since leaving Paddington, set at caution against him. *Peter W. Gray*

Christmas Eve 1959 at the east end of Newton Abbot station. A nice, bright, clear night, the signal lights crisp and visible from far off. Remember then, the loyal 'lampy' who kept strictly to the seven-day rota throughout Newton Abbot station, from East box to Aller Junction, if not Hackney Yard box as well, keeping the seven-day-burning lamps always alight. On this gantry alone there are a dozen lamps to clean, trim, fill and carry out from lamp hut to site. The driver of No 4179 is grateful and looks forward keenly, ready for the 'off'. *Peter W. Gray*

How do you think the footplatemen got their trains through on time when faced with fog? (And maybe a leaking steam gland to make the murk worse.) Trains need a mile in which to stop. Oil lamps, dim or invisible on tall masts, were the driver's — and passengers' — security. Where to look to see them in the clag? The tracks curved and signals were by no means always straight ahead. These men relied on their courage, confidence in their route knowledge — and, arguably, nerves of steel.
Peter W. Gray/Colour-Rail

John Ashman, a good friend to me for many years, was keen to have fine signals in his pictures. Here he has carefully contrived to make two gantries seem like one spectacular gantry. D1056 *Western Sultan* is on the down relief line passing below Reading East Main's down relief outer home, with West Main's distant at caution below. The down relief to down main signal is to the right and to the left is East Main's up relief line advanced starter with Reading Power Station box's distant below. The other set of signals control the up main line over Reading New Junction, about ¾mile east of the station, to the Southern. From left to right they read: up main with Power Station distant below; up SR passenger loop and calling-on arm below; up Southern with Kennet spur distant fixed at caution and calling-on arm below. The facing point to the Southern can be seen; this is motor-worked. To the right is an electrically-operated ground signal, backing from down main to down Southern.
John H. Ashman FRPS

Reading as I knew it in 1951. No 4036 *Queen Elizabeth* steps proudly out of Platform 5 and away up the main past the East Main box. This box contained a 115-lever frame installed in 1896 and a miniature lever power frame installed in 1940 to work the New Junction ¼ mile towards London. The splendid wooden signals are the down relief line inner home and West Main's distant with a calling-on arm below that. The left hand arm routed into No 6 bay, the right hand arm signalled from down relief to down goods. There is also a backing arm low on the post. John Ashman was standing between the down main line and the line to the Southern. In the distance, the down main signals are lowered for an express which will shortly be brushing his right elbow unless he moves! People looked after themselves in those days; no orange vests or lookouts. *John Ashman FRPS*

No 7921 *Edstone Hall*, running 'F' headcode (3-2 on the signalman's bell) at Reading East Main's inner homes with a train of empty coal wagons, signalled from the down relief line into the down goods running loop at Reading East Main. This signal replaced the one in the previous view and was erected on 22 July 1957, when the track was rearranged to give access to No 10 bay from the down relief. The signal second from left routes into No 10 bay, the next routes down relief with West Main's distant below, and the right hand routes into No 6 bay. There are calling-on arms below. In the right background is East Main's down main inner home with West Main's splitting distants below for the Bristol or Westbury lines. Below the Western embankment on the right is the Southern station's goods yard. Taken c1963.
John Ashman FRPS

No 5086 *Viscount Horne*, a Worcester engine, going home with the 1.45pm Paddington, crossing the Berks & Hants line junction at Reading Main Line West in the summer of 1954. *Colour-Rail*

The famous signal gantry at Reading West Main. From the left there are: up main to up main platform starting with East Main's 'slipping distant' below; up main starting and East Main distant, pulled off; down main to down relief line starting; down main starting with West Junction's distant; down main to engine shed; down main to Berks & Hants line with Oxford Road Junction's distant; bays 1, 2 and 3 with platform indicator and calling-on arm. Low down on the left hand upright of the gantry two backing arms be partly seen. Taken c1957. Note that cast iron finials are used to decorate even the gantry uprights. *John Ashman FRPS*

The magnificent interior of Reading Main Line West signalbox in 1960. This was the largest mechanical lever frame on the GWR or Western Region, with 210 levers; there were spaces for another 12. There were two other mechanical boxes of similar size: Newton Abbot East with a frame numbered to 206 and Cardiff Queen Street North, numbered to 200. The signalbox was a specially decorative design in red and yellow brick with ornate ridge tiles and finials, opened about 1896. The original frame was replaced by the one seen here in 1943. In the left hand corner, short levers 31, 32 and 33 operated powered points for the diesel depot. Next to them, levers 34 and 36 are reversed, bolting the up main to up relief and the up relief to up main facers on the big scissors crossing. Standing by the levers is Signalman Ken Morton, at the centre of the frame is Signalman Blake talking to Inspector Tom Rixon, and the booking lad is in his enclosure recording the time and the message from each one of a dozen bells, as well as sending and receiving train running information and making enquiries about train running on behalf of the signalmen. Three signalmen attend to 70 levers each, some bells and no telephones but the booking boy attends to all bells and telephones. *Adrian Vaughan Collection*

Ken Morton is about to give 'Line clear' on the up main line to Reading West Junction. The other signalboxes in communication with Main Line West were West Goods, Main Line East and Oxford Road Junction. Until June 1959 there was also a Middle box working with Main Line West. Note the double scissors crossover referred to in the previous caption. *Adrian Vaughan Collection*

No 4607 is crossing over the Salisbury line junctions and passing the 99-lever Westbury South box with a train of tar tanks for Cranmore, plus a single truck of coal, on 13 July 1964. *R. C. Riley*

No 7813 Freshford Manor canters into Cholsey & Moulsford station in May 1965, passing the GWR wartime design of tubular steel bracket steel signal which carries Cholsey's up relief starting and up relief to up main starting signals.
Ron Price/Adrian Vaughan Collection

Oxford was one of the busiest junctions on the Western Region. The largest signalbox, the North box, had 99 levers and was manned by two men and a boy — a third man being drafted in as traffic regulator at peak times. On 15 August 1959 No 4956 *Plowden Hall* is leaving (at 8.53am if it was on time) from the down platform on the 7.10am Paddington-Wolverhampton via Banbury. It has 11 or 12 on and has left two carriages behind, attached to the pilot at the south end of the station. On the down main is a '90xxx' 'WD' waiting to go to shed. *R. C. Riley*

All is well with No 7006 *Lydford Castle* and the fireman takes his ease, waiting for 'right away' on the 2.7pm to Banbury on 3 March 1961. The wooden engine shed on the left dates from about 1852 and remained in use until 1966, the only major improvement in that time being the replacement of the coaling stage in 1944. On the footpath a homeward bound guard enjoys the mighty 'Castle' while on the gantry the Signal & Telegraph lineman is adjusting the electric motor of Oxford North Junction's distant signal and his assistant does the sensible thing and admires the view below him. *David Anderson*

On 19 April 1956 No 6974 *Bryngwyn Hall* stands at Oxford Station South's up home signals and the fireman is putting plenty on in preparation for a sharp run to Paddington. This is Oxford's answer to the 'Bristolian', the 5.35pm to Paddington, booked 60min for the 63½ miles with seven or eight coaches. The train originated as the 2.15 Wolverhampton, remanned with Oxford men at Oxford. The schedule dated back to GWR days and, like the 'Bristolian', it was discontinued in 1939 and reinstated in the summer of 1954. The nationalised railwaymen entered into the race against time with as much skill in 1956 as 1936. The first emblem of the nationalised railway, seen here on the tender of *Bryngwyn Hall*, expressed well the postwar ruggedness and pride

in the job. My friend, Oxford based Driver Charlie Turner was not in the link working this train but was keen enough to ask a friend who was, George Theobald, to swop turns with him and he had five days on the 5.35 with No 5039 *Rhuddlan Castle* . Oxford has an awkward exit for half a mile before a driver can 'set sail', and after eight miles he must shut off and coast through Appleford and around the sharply curved Didcot avoiding line, down to the 40mph restriction over the junctions onto the up main — the 'Silver Road'. To keep time, speed had to be in the 80s for long periods. The running was legendary and was regularly timed by lay enthusiasts, the record being 54½ minutes. *R. C. Riley*

The Gara Bridge signalman exchanges electric key tokens with the fireman of No 4561, running light to Brent at 2pm on 29 April 1961. *Peter W. Gray*

2. Plymouth Relief Signalman

The first signalman's job to be advertised after Larry had become a porter-signalman was Tigley. Tigley box was near the 225½ Milepost from Paddington (via Bristol), 2¾ miles west of Totnes and 1¾ miles east of Rattery. The ruling gradient from Totnes to Rattery, a distance of 4½ miles, was given in the GWR Service Timetable as 1 in 47. Thereafter gradients were relatively reasonable — all in three figures at any rate — for 12 miles up to the steep drop at Hemerdon. Tigley was there simply to divide the section and thus increase line capacity on the steep gradient out of the Dart Valley from Totnes.

Tigley was a Class 4 signalbox with nine levers, its signalmen earning £5 6s for a 'flat week' of 44 hours, one week in three. They got more for a week of nights or for working seven days including Sunday, again one week in three. The signalbox had no running water, no electricity and a lavatory which was at any convenient spot in the copse behind the box. Washing water came from the rainwater butt and drinking water in a milk churn on the buffer beam of the Totnes banker; having assisted a freight up to Rattery, it would return light engine and stop at Tigley to put off the churn.

The box was open almost continuously, closing only from 10pm Saturday to 6am Sunday. It was 21½ miles east of Plymouth by rail. On early turn there was no train which would get Larry to work on time but he was determined to start as soon as possible as a signalman and so he bought a 1935 Ford 8 which cost him a whopping £175 — just to get himself to work on early turn. On late turn and nights he took the train. Petrol was rationed and he could not get enough to use the car on all three shifts.

Larry kept two bicycles; one under the box at Totnes, the other on the station at North Road. He did not take a bike on the train because he would have been charged for it. He got off the train at Totnes and cycled up the hilly road about 3¾ miles to Tigley. When he got back to Plymouth at the end of a late turn, round about 11.30, he had another bike on which to cycle home to St Budeaux. At the end of his night shift he had to pedal hard down the road to Totnes to catch the 11.50pm Paddington mail and passenger express. It was a lot of work to get to and from work but it was no more than many other dedicated railwaymen did.

Larry was waiting on the platform one dark morning and the 11.50pm rolled in double-headed — a pair of 'Kings'. This was contrary to the safety regulations so he went to the crew of the pilot engine and asked, 'How long have 'Kings' been allowed to double-head over this line then?'

The driver looked at him pityingly — he was only a Traffic Department man, after all. 'That's a 'Castle' behind us,' he said confidently.

'Oh, I see,' said Larry, knowing better. So he went to the crew of the train engine and asked the same question and got the same answer. 'I think you'd better get off and have a look,' said Larry. There was great surprise and consternation because for the sake of the viaducts it was not permitted to run over them with two 'Kings'. Anyhow, the men decided that, as they hadn't yet fallen off a viaduct or collapsed one, they would go on to Plymouth at reduced speed. Not long after this incident the regulation was abolished.

Totnes signalbox soon became well known to Larry. It was a handsome box inside and out and was especially interesting to work because it dealt with the bank engines for Rattery and for Dainton and also had the Ashburton branch. There were seven signals to lower for the up or down main lines and even more levers to pull if you had to set the road for the platform loops. On the Ashburton branch, trains were worked by the train staff and ticket system. The Totnes signalman worked with Staverton, using a telegraph instrument

◄ D812 *Royal Naval Reserve 1859-1959*, almost brand new, has a load of 13 coaches on the down 'Cornish Riviera Ltd' and is assisted past Tigley box by one of the oldest 'Halls', No 4905 *Barton Hall*, on 11 September 1960. *Peter W. Gray*

installed by the South Devon Railway in 1872. He 'asked the road' to Staverton, '3-1-3' on the bell, and when permission had been given by Staverton for the train to leave, he either unlocked the ticket box with the train staff and took out a ticket as the driver's authority to enter the single line, or he gave him the actual staff.

Working at Tigley through the magnificent summer of 1949, Larry had a fabulous view northwards to Dartmoor and a constant procession of magnificent trains either crashing great guns up the hill or rattling by helter-skelter down the bank. The ARGO TransAcord Recording Company have preserved the sounds of Tigley for all time. Larry has the pictures in his head. One very fine day, the permanent way gang were standing shoulder to shoulder in a line along the north edge of the embankment, admiring the view. Larry noticed them as he was 'pulling off' and as he pulled his starting signal, they all shot off down the bank, hell for leather. 'I wonder what's up with them?' thought Larry and got on with his work. Later on they came trooping past the box and Larry hung out. 'What did you go chasing after, now?'

'We didn't go chasing after nothing. We was all standing with our heels on the wire of your signal and when you pulled off it lifted us an' threw us down the bank.'

Getting to and from Tigley was really very difficult and made for a long working day or night. In November 1949 a temporary job as signalman came up at Bickleigh, due to one of the signalman there having his leg amputated. This box was a grade lower than Tigley and there was no night shift, so wages were £5 2s a week but it was only eight miles from St Budeaux — cycling distance for a good man — so Larry applied for the vacancy and got it. The box opened at 5.15am each day. When he was on this shift he got up at 3am, drank a glass of milk and set off pedalling the eight miles to Bickleigh. The first half was decidedly uphill, from St Budeaux, 50ft above sea level, up over Crownhill crossroads, past the barracks and eventually to the 500ft summit on Bickleigh Down. This starting time gave him half an hour recovery time in case of bad weather or a puncture. If all went well he got to work at 4.45am. It was a matter of honour to get to work on time.

One morning, shortly after he had turned off the main Tavistock road and was cycling down towards Bickleigh, he ran into a herd of Dartmoor ponies in the road. He slammed on his brakes and tried to get through them but they moved off ahead of him and all he could do was follow. Going so slowly, his dynamo-driven headlamp did not work, so he could see nothing but only hear about a dozen unshod ponies softly clip-clopping ahead. They had nowhere to turn off and trotted ahead of him in the dark with the soft pad-plat, pad-plat of unshod hooves. All through sleeping Bickleigh village they went, filling the road with stout, dark bodies and the sound of drumming, padding hooves, never deviating and Larry in the rear unable to get past. As they passed the gates and guardroom of the Royal Marines camp, the few lights gave a silhouette of dark rumps, swishing tails and flopping manes, trotting purposefully they knew not where, through the night. Leaving the camp behind, the collective conscience of the herd began to work and the consensus was that they should get out of his way at the very next turning. Half a mile beyond the village the road for the station turned left and up this the ponies obligingly swerved and cantered hard away but, finding Larry was *still* behind them, they dashed into the station forecourt and milled around, blocking Larry's way in.

His half-hour grace came in handy that morning and he was able to send '5-5-5', 'Opening Signalbox', to Marsh Mills just on time.

There was no switching-out instrument; when Bickleigh was closed, the line was effectively closed. The man at Marsh Mills acknowledged '5-5-5' and held his tapper down on the last stroke so that Larry could test that the staff instrument was in order by taking out a staff and returning it at once. Larry would then 'hold down' for the Marsh Mills man to test. This done, Marsh Mills 'asked clear' for the Tavistock goods. Larry gave a release for the electric train staff and then got on with lighting his handlamp, the Tilley paraffin pressure lamp and then the box stove.

The 3¾ miles of line from Marsh Mills rose up the Plym Valley at 1 in 90, steepening to 1 in 60 nearer Bickleigh. Through the station the line was level before continuing the 1 in 60 climb on the 3½ miles to Yelverton. The engines were working hard and the goods trains were often banked in the rear. They could be heard from far off in the early morning stillness but they could not be seen until they were close, owing to the curvature of the approach cutting to the station. Permitted speed for electric train staff changing by hand was 10mph but the engines were hard at work and their drivers keen to take advantage of the level length through the station and so the heavy iron staffs with their protruding brass rings were snatched between the fireman and signalman at double the authorised speed.

The first train of the early shift, the 5.15 Laira Junction, was banked in the rear. To exchange the staff by hand, in the dark, as the train stormed through was a work of art and confidence. Larry stood in the six-foot between the up and down platform lines, holding the staff upright in his right hand, shining his handlamp on it with his left hand. The fireman of the bank engine leant out over the cabside with his right hand empty, extended as far forward from his left hand as he could, while holding in his left hand the staff, hanging downwards in his fingers. The fireman grabbed the staff from Larry's right hand and a split second later, Larry's empty right hand grabbed the other staff from the fireman.

The staff instrument at Bickleigh was worn out and sometimes would not work, necessitating pilot working. Eventually an 'occupation' was arranged to remove the instruments and replace them with electric key token instruments. Jack Pascoe came out from Plymouth to act as pilotman but he missed his turning, crossed the line and headed off up a steep hill on to the moor. He carried on, and on, and finally met an early-rising farm worker. 'Wer's th' station to?' asked Jack.

'Straight on down the hill.'

Dainton Sidings signalbox was built by Saxby & Farmer for the South Devon Railway and was brought into use about 1874. The box had a frame of 17 levers. The signalman's first sight of down trains was through the 264yd tunnel. The summit of the climb was within the tunnel, so he saw their exhaust first, then the chimney, before the whole thing was lost in the darkness of the tunnel. Loose-coupled, unbraked down goods trains stopped by the box to allow the guard to pin down a proportion of the wagon handbrakes, to assist braking down the 1 in 37 towards Totnes. This created a severe bottleneck. On 23 June 1957 No 5376 is hauling a Plymouth-Exeter stopping train, probably the 4.20pm Penzance, 7.10pm Plymouth, and is passing an elevated mirror attached to a tall, white post. The mirror was provided to enable the signalman to see the tail lamp of up trains when the view would be blocked by a down train passing the box, or standing outside the box, or the smoke of a train hanging thickly on a wet day. Note the well-made, illuminated '40' speed restriction sign, mounted on signal post timber. A new signalbox was built here — 'Dainton Tunnel' — in February 1965 and this was abolished under automation in 1985. *R. C. Riley*

Dainton Bank, westbound, is two miles long. It begins at 1 in 98 and includes a mile at around 1 in 44, with a section of 1 in 36 within that. No 6023 King Edward II with the 10-coach 3.30pm Paddington is coming up the 1 in 44 in June 1958, at perhaps 10-12mph, which is about what the schedule required. Dainton box up starting signal is at danger while at the rear of the train can be seen Stoneycombe's up distant off and Dainton's down distant signal off. *Peter W. Gray/Colour-Rail*

Jack kept on and on some more and finally recognised the village of Ivybridge. The expertise slipped that morning.

Larry was at Bickleigh until January 1951 when a Class 4 signalman's job came up at Mount Gould Junction. This was at the south end of the Plymouth Laira triangle, working with the Southern Region Plymouth Friary 'A' box to the south, except when Friary Junction was switched in to let trains into or out of the Sutton Harbour branch. To the north, on the Western Region main line, Mount Gould worked with Lipson Junction at the Plymouth end and Laira Junction on the main line east of Lipson.

When Hemerdon box, a Class 3, became vacant in August, Larry applied for it and took over the duties on 15 September. His wages were now £5 10s a week with extra pay for nights and Sundays. Hemerdon really was a lovely place to work, with a lot of operating responsibility *and* superb views north to Dartmoor and that beautiful hill feature Hemerdon Ball — over whose flank the railway climbed from Plympton.

Eastwards the line contoured around the hills to Cornwood box, often switched out, and Ivybridge. The line westwards went down into the Plym Valley on a 1 in 42 gradient for 2½ miles to Plympton. Down freight trains took 10 minutes from Ivybridge to Hemerdon. There they stopped at a stop board, by the advanced starting signal on level track, in order for the guard to pin down brakes for the precipitous descent. This operation took six minutes. A further nine minutes was required for the train to clear the section at Plympton. Two minutes was allowed for the train to stop at the board and a minute to restart — 28 minutes in all from Ivybridge to Plympton.

The job of regulating or 'margining' goods trains up and down the incline, in between the passenger trains, was the responsibility of the Hemerdon signalman. Hemerdon had an up and a down loop holding 58 wagons. The trap points at each exit were fitted with facing point bolts so that passenger trains could be put in. He put trains aside according to how he perceived the train service was working and after making due enquiries of the other signalmen. On one occasion Larry put a down local passenger into his loop to allow the 'Cornish Riviera', running late, to get by.

Up trains hauled by tank engines had to have longer margins to Brent loop than those hauled by tender engines, because the former would stop for water at Wrangaton. So if the requisite time ahead of the next passenger train was not there, Hemerdon would put the freight in his up loop or, if that was full, refuse to have it out of Plympton loop. If Tavistock Junction 'asked clear' up the main to Plympton for a goods, Plympton would 'get the road' from Hemerdon before returning 'Line clear' to Tavistock Junction. Bank engines were put to the rear of a goods train while it stood in the loop at Plympton and the Plympton man would need to know that the banker was in place before he 'asked clear' for it to Hemerdon. The ordinary railwaymen took a great deal of responsibility for running the trains.

In those days the loops all along the line were in constant use and the signalmen liaised with each other. The signalman at Brent would ring Hemerdon: 'Can I let this one here down to you after the next fast? Totnes is all blocked up and wants to get rid of one to me.' Hemerdon might refuse and then the Totnes and the Brent men would come on the 'bus line and hound the Hemerdon man to let one go out of his loop — but they would not have to answer for the delay if Hemerdon miscalculated and so the Hemerdon man would have to stand his ground. 'Margining' was a cross between the official times and a work of art.

One superb summer day, an electricity board man was working in the field behind the signalbox. He was singing away up his pole and the song came drifting in through Larry's open window as he worked. After a while the man came into the box for some hot water to make tea but Larry had a pot full and some sandwiches and shared it all with the man. The electricity man was very interested in the signalbox and all its equipment and workings, asking many questions, obviously fascinated — dull of soul would he be who was not. Plympton asked up a '3-1', 'Is line clear for a stopping passenger train?' The bell rang as clear as the bright, blue sky. Then the 'two beats' — 'on line'. It was a perfect, still day, and a few seconds later the sound of the engine barking away from Plympton station came clearly up the hill, still 2½ miles away. The electricity board man 'supposed' that Larry could tell what type of engine was approaching. As luck would have it, Larry could — and not only the type but its name and number! The man expressed a degree of scepticism. 'Oh yes,' said Larry, 'this here is No 1000 *County of Middlesex*.' No doubt the electricity man thought he was having his leg pulled. The ripping sound of the exhaust, yet weirdly hollow, got louder and louder until under the bridge burst the hulking form of a 'County' — *Middlesex*. Well, the layman was deeply impressed, having no idea that No 1000 had the only double-chimney exhaust arrangement on the railway and was thus perfectly recognisable.

Hemerdon Bank was a serious matter for steam engines, especially those with a green fire and cold cylinders, newly started on their journey and fresh off shed. Up passenger and goods trains stalled fairly regularly, so much so that a lineside telephone was provided in the wood, halfway up the bank, to enable the guard of a stalled train to contact Plympton signalbox for banking assistance. Someone had thoughtlessly planted a wood on both sides of the line about halfway up and, in autumn, leaves on the rails brought trains to a stand. But in any season, trains stalled occasionally on the bank, from being short of steam, from the mistake of a guard in calculating the load as 'single horse' or from the optimism of the driver thinking that he could take a slight overload without a banker.

After 'Train entering section' from Plympton, the Hemerdon signalman could follow the train's progress, the exhaust becoming louder and slower to a steady four-beats-to-the-bar and then, if they were unlucky, the sound of a brief slip, silence as the driver shut off steam and then the slower beat as steam came on again and way was lost. The signalman listened carefully — and most signalmen became quite expert in judging the odds on the train making it to the summit. If the sound stopped altogether the signalmen at both ends of the section were already prepared for it: 'That up one's stuck on the bank, you'd better get the banker out from Tavi Yard.' When the guard rang in he could be told that the matter was in hand and to walk back to meet the oncoming banking engine and conduct it to the rear of his train. When the bank engine passed Plympton, two beats on the bell was sent to Hemerdon and Hemerdon did not then give 'Train out of section' until the train and the banking engine had got clear of the section.

One day Larry was on duty when the signal painting gang turned up. They came in a lorry because they had to transport their ladders and materials to the site but for the rest of their stay they had to make their own way to the box. The lorry was the only one belonging to the Signal & Telegraph Department in the district and was needed for other jobs. Sometimes they walked from Cornwood, not quite two miles, and in the evenings got a lift down into Plymouth on some convenient goods train. They were there to paint the signals, signal levers and signalbox itself, the latter for only the second time since it was opened in 1931. The foreman was an older man called Alec, who

was well known for taking the easiest jobs on account of his age and elevated position. He gave his gang the rougher work and then said he was going to paint the up distant post — he could see it from the track by the box and thought it was close enough to be an easy walk. It was 826yd in fact, and Alec was happy with that. At the end of the day they all walked back to Plympton. They were back the following day and Alec announced he was going to paint the down distant. 'You feeling energetic today then, Alec?' asked Larry. 'It's a long walk out to that.'

'Oh, no — your distants are quite close here. I can walk out to 'e.'

'Well, have it your own way then, Alec.' He said goodbye to his gang at 8.30 and was not seen again until he trudged into the box at about 3.30 and slumped wearily into the chair.

'Where've you been?' they asked. 'We was thinking of sending out a search party.'

'I walked an' walked to get out to it,' gasped Alec, 'An' then I had to paint it and then walk all the way back again. That down distant's a lot further out than your up one.'

'One thousand, four hundred and ninety-seven yards, Alec!' said Larry. 'And now you've got to walk the best part of three miles to Plympton.'

No 5558, standing beside the 27-lever Gara Bridge box, has a coach to strengthen the usual 'B set' on the 11.15 (SO) Kingsbridge to Brent on 6 August 1960. Perhaps on Saturdays people had time to take advantage of the 3s 9d (19p) excursion ticket to Plymouth and were crowding the train. *Hugh Ballantyne*

No 6834 *Dummer Grange* blows off steam with the regular Laira-Avonmouth return empty box vans, nearing the summit of the eastbound climb of Dainton. The train is therefore lighter than it looks — and the banking engine is working, out of sight, at the rear. For eastbound trains, Dainton Bank was only 1¾ miles long, and in theory less steep than the westbound climb, starting at 1 in 260 but soon rising at 1 in 76, 55 and finally 1 in 37. However, the route was very serpentine, which effectively made the gradient worse than the westbound climb. Dainton's down starting signal is behind the engine, on the 'wrong' side of the line.
Peter W. Gray/Colour-Rail

An array of splendid signals seen from the noon Kingswear-Manchester express; Exeter West up main starting signals on 22 August 1959. The arm, No 4, is lowered for Platform 5, the up main platform. Arm 6, to the right, is for the up middle Platform 4 and the other main arm is worked by lever 5 for the up relief line, Platform 6. The extreme left arm, No 10, routes to up goods or locomotive shed, the other, No 11, to the goods sidings. The locomotive is No 5976 *Ashwicke Hall.* We are indebted to Peter Gray for taking this photograph and keeping meticulous records of each view. *Peter W. Gray*

No 34059 *Sir Archibald Sinclair* passes a '28xx'-hauled goods in the down loop at Hemerdon and covers Hemerdon box in a haze of smoke. The loop held 58 wagons plus the engine and van but it was also permitted to hold passenger trains. The facing point bolt at the trap point, essential if passenger trains are to pass over it, together with the 4ft arm of the loop starting signal, can be seen. 1955. *Peter Barlow/ Adrian Vaughan Collection*

No 6827 *Llanfrecha Grange* barks crisply away from Exeter St Davids on a parcels train on 23 June 1962, passing the 131-lever West box (now preserved in working order at Crewe Heritage Centre) and a fine GWR backing signal. Coming the other way, signalled into No 6 Platform, is a '6959' class 'Hall' with a Goodrington to Southern Region excursion. This will be signalled through the station to the east side of the Middle box. The 'Hall' will then reverse it through the crossover to the down main line and into the down middle — Platform 3. The Southern engine, which will be waiting in the incline spur at the West box, will then drop on to the train. *R. C. Riley*

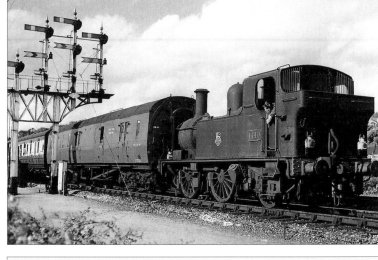

Longdown, showing the Webb & Thompson large staff instruments with the ganger's key control instrument between them. The signalling bells are above their instruments. The closest one works to Exeter City Basin Junction, the other to Christow. Below the City Basin bell are two ancient telephones. At top right are the lamp repeaters for the up and down distant signals. The signalbox had a frame of nine levers. 9 November 1959. *Peter W. Gray*

On a glorious summer day in June 1956, No 1440, as station pilot, is standing in the sun on the up main, having drawn a train of empty coaches out of the station, over the Exe Bridge, on the up main. The fireman is peering intently forwards and down, waiting to see the ground signal move and the shunter's signal to come forward. The Exeter West signalman, who was paid as a Special B, had a terrific job as he dealt with all this shunting, engines on and off shed and main line trains. The gantry was erected in 1942, carries West box up starting signals and has five posts: three for Platforms 4, 5 and 6 with Exeter Middle's distants and West's calling-on arms, and two short posts with arms for up goods loop and engine shed. *David Anderson*

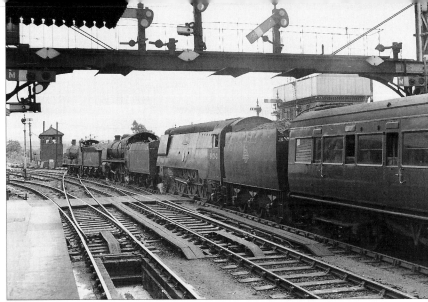

On a cold, wet February day in 1958 the indefatigable Peter Gray was keeping watch at Exeter and photographed No 5078 *Beaufort* pulling out with the down 'Torbay Express'. Standing alongside Platform 3 is No 5024 *Carew Castle* with the 3.5pm stopping train, distributing passengers from the 'Torbay Express' to all intermediate stations to Kingswear. Exeter West was one of the very busiest boxes on the Western Region and, to maintain the highest rating for pay, was normally manned by one signalman and a booking boy. A second man was drafted in on summer Saturdays. It had a 114-lever frame dating from 1912 — which was becoming worn out from constant use and which would be replaced in 1959. Note the centre-pivoted home signal routeing to the down main and marked accordingly. Platform 3 was used by all up Southern trains and the junction to the Southern station can be seen crossing in front of No 5078. There is a trap point in front of No 5024, hidden by the platform, to prevent a conflicting movement from taking place. *Peter W. Gray*

The Webb & Thompson staffs between Longdown and City Basin had bayonet fitting lugs to enable a pick-up/set-down carrier to be used. This was by no means the case with all staffs of this type. Here, the fireman of No 1469, hauling the 12.40pm Newton Abbot to Exeter via Heathfield and Longdown, is about put the carrier over the 'cow's horn' at Exeter City Basin Junction on 18 January 1958. The reason for using the carrier here was that the signalbox was on the main line embankment and there was a deep valley between it and the Teign Valley line embankment. A footbridge was provided across the gap but the signalman, dealing also with the busy main line and the branch to City Basin, might not have been able to go and take the staff from the train crew at the moment of the train's passing. *Peter W. Gray*

Obviously a Southern train leaves Exeter St Davids Platform 3 for Central station on 9 August 1958. The locomotives are: '700' class No 30317; 'U' No 31610 and No 34060 *25 Squadron*. The train is the 11.35am Plymouth Friary to Waterloo. It was breaking local instructions to have three engines on the front of a train but, at Exeter, rules sometimes bent under pressure of work. Note how the various signal arms are clearly marked with the route they apply to. The down main is the central track and the signal routeing from it to the Southern is obscured by the awning. Above the Pacific's tender can be seen two backing arms flanking a running signal. This applied to Platform 4, up middle line, which could be used for down line departures. *Peter W. Gray*

No 1451 at Exeter St Davids on 5 February 1961, waiting to leave the up bay, Platform 2, with the Tiverton train. In the distance is the 91-lever Exeter Middle box, with a Southern 'W' class 2-6-4 tank standing in the bank engine spur. To get No 1451 and train to the up main will require the signalman to make about 16 lever movements and the same number to restore the route when the train has left. *R. C. Riley*

In August 1961 a severe collapse of an embankment between Partney & Chirton and Lavington occurred, entirely severing the West of England main line for a few days and causing some bizarre diversions. Here at Exeter St Davids No 5055 *Earl of Eldon* is standing at the down main platform with a Swansea-Penzance express while, half-hidden by the gantry, the 'Warship'-hauled 'Cornish Riviera Express' is standing at No 3 Platform, to travel to London via the Southern Region as far as Basingstoke and there rejoin the Western Region. *Peter W. Gray/Colour-Rail*

No 5090 *Earl of Dunraven* whistles melodiously as it approaches Exeter St Davids with the board off for the down main platform. In the background can be seen Exeter East box. The signals are Exeter Middle's down homes with Exeter West's distants below (the electric motors can be seen) and Middle box's calling-on signal below them. The signal for No 1 (bay) Platform is hidden behind wagons on the right. The left-hand home signal routes to Platform 3; the distant signal below this is fixed at 'caution' because of the low speed permitted over the facing turn-out. The tallest post carries the signals for the down main, with a working distant signal whose electric motor can be seen to the left of the post. The distant signal below the lowered arm is also workable, in spite of the 20mph turn-out ahead; this is provided to prove to the driver and guard of a nonstop train carrying a slip coach for Exeter that the road is clear through and that it is safe to slip the coach. Taken circa 1953. *John Ashman FRPS*

Where trains were permitted to run over either arm of a junction at 40mph or more, a working distant signal for both routes was provided. These stood beside the up main at Aynho Junction, the left-hand arm directing to Bicester and the other towards the Oxford route. The train hauled by No 7012 *Barry Castle* is the 9.35 Bournemouth West-Manchester, the 'Pines Express', in the first year after it was diverted from the Somerset & Dorset route. Seen on 15 April 1963. *Hugh Ballantyne*

Leamington South box up platform and up main home signals, with Leamington South Junction's distant signals below. In the background an LMS tubular steel utility job forms the down home for Leamington Avenue (LMS) station and the tower of All Saints, the parish church, is behind that. *R. C. Riley*

No 5070 *Sir Daniel Gooch* on the 10.10am Paddington drifts through the down middle at Exeter St Davids with the 'back boards' on, in June 1963, admired, perhaps, by the fireman on No 34072 *257 Squadron*. This engine is also heading to Plymouth. A legacy of railway history. *Peter W. Gray/Colour-Rail*

The view from the signalbox of the 1.10pm Dulverton-Tiverton two-car auto being propelled out of Bampton station by No 1468. Even as late as 26 June 1960, the station and the ancient train were kept in the best GWR state of paint and repair. What a shocking shame that it had to go — and therefore all the craftsmanship and employment that was a part of it. *Peter W. Gray*

No 6866 *Morfa Grange* is running on the down main line at Moreton Cutting's advanced starting signal with a Birmingham train on 4 July 1953. Moreton Cutting's down main and down relief line advanced starting signals are cleared, allowing access into Didcot East Junction's section. The latter's down main to down avoiding line distant is cleared. The other distant signals on this bracket route to down relief line or down main. The train will be crossing all four tracks at East Junction and East Junction's down relief line distants are at caution for the train signalled on that line. East Junction could accept the latter train from Moreton Cutting because it had an outer home signal protecting the crossing movement more than 440yd to the rear of the junction. *R. C. Riley*

Early morning departure from the up main platform at Didcot in 1962. The rear coach is passing Didcot East Junction's up main home signal; to the left is the up relief line (URL) home. Next left is a cluster of three: East Junction's down avoiding line starting signal, No 25, with Didcot North Junction's distant below and the arm routeing into the down avoiding line goods loop; the up avoiding line home and a bracket signal routeing from up avoiding to up main or up avoiding goods loop to up goods loop. Nearer the camera, on the left, are two wooden post bracket signals with ringed arms. The left-hand signal forms the exit signal from the engine shed to spur or URL; the lowered arm allows access from Didcot Yard sidings to the spur and its partner from sidings to URL. *David Anderson*

Plymouth North Road station from the west, 22 August 1956. The original main line into Millbay station and the docks is on the right; the line into Cornwall is on the left. The West signalbox originally occupied a site on the bridge, behind the bracket signal at the centre of the view. After the bridge was widened in November 1938, its locking frame was removed, the wooden building was jacked up and, with rollers beneath it, was moved to the site seen in this view. During World War 2 it had a concrete blast wall around the outside, up to floor level. When the young Larry was visiting the box and saw the inspector or stationmaster approaching, he climbed on to the wall from the rear window and dropped off the wall, down the embankment and on to the road. *BR(W)/Larry Crosier Collection*

3. 'Right Away the Boat Train'

One sunlit evening, after a beautiful day, a Goodrington-North Road excursion came crawling into Hemerdon. All the boards were off, so Larry knew something was wrong and went to the window. The driver shouted as he passed, 'Cows on the line!' and pointed back down the train. After the train had gone Larry could see the animals on the track by his down home signal — and coming his way. He phoned Control to rouse the ganger, Pen Turpin, from his house in Cornwood but working people did not have telephones in their houses in those days, so that would be a lengthy business and so Larry decided to switch his box out and get on to the line, so as to prevent the cows from going down the bank towards Plympton. He told Plympton and Ivybridge what he was going to do and why. Plympton and Ivybridge would then have to stop trains and warn the drivers to go forward under caution; that would not be difficult for those starting from Plympton up a 1 in 41 gradient.

Larry walked along to the cows and started to try to find the broken place in the fence to pass them through into the field. The fence was made of taut strands of wire with light steel notched verticals to hold the wires apart. He had been there for some time and trains were creeping past in the twilight when Pen Turpin arrived. He was understandably cross and said he'd soon have these so-and-so cows off the line. But neither of the men could find where the fence

was broken and one of the cows took a dislike to Pen pushing her around and lost *her* temper, charged at Pen and pinned him against the fence, bending one of the steel verticals. 'Larry! Larry! Get this cow off me!' cried Pen in some alarm. The only thing for it was to slack the wires off at the straining post, let the whole lot into someone's field and then strain it up again. It would do until morning to get the line clear. For 30 years afterwards that steel upright remained bent and Larry always looked out for it should he be passing in a train.

One night a down parcels train stopped at Hemerdon and the driver told Larry that he had had a red light waved at him from a bridge between Ivybridge and Hemerdon. As the next down train was the TPO, Larry thought someone might be trying to rob the Royal Mail and had flagged down the wrong train. He phoned Control and the TPO was put into the platform line at Totnes. The BR police were informed and they searched the affected portion of the line. Nothing was found — except that, where a piece of a bridge parapet had been taken down for rebuilding, a red lamp, threaded on a piece of rope, had been placed in the gap to warn road users of the danger and this was dancing merrily in the wind.

Larry was keen to work as many boxes as possible and, when a vacancy arose at Plymouth North Road for a Class 2 reliefman in the No 2 District, he applied for it. He was then using a motorbike to get to Hemerdon and would call in at

No 5017 *The Gloucestershire Regiment* hurries down Sapperton Bank towards Brimscombe station with the 11.5am Paddington-Gloucester express on 25 August 1962. On the left is Brimscombe East signalbox up starting signal with St Mary's Crossing distant below and below that a calling-on arm. The banking engine shed dates from the opening of the line in 1845. The line rises from here for 4 miles; the gradient begins at 1 in 100 but soon steepens to 1 in 75/60/50 to the mouth of Sapperton Tunnel and continues at 1 in 90 under the Cotswold Ridge for 1,860yd. This was one of my favourite places. Goods trains were routinely banked up here in steam days, as well as passenger trains as required. *R. C. Riley*

Half a mile up the bank was St Mary's Crossing. The signalbox dates from about 1875. Long before 1936 it had been reduced to groundframe status. It had only a home and distant signal in each direction and on the up line its home signal was also Brimscombe East's advanced starting signal, giving headroom for a long goods train to pull forward, clear of the banking engine siding at Brimscombe. 125 years after its opening, the building is still carrying out its crossing control function, released from Gloucester Panel. No 1425 is on the famous 'Chalford auto' on 25 June 1962. *R. C. Riley*

Plympton station every third Sunday on his way to 12-hour night shift, to collect clean lever-dusters and any other stores. Calling in there one Sunday evening, the stationmaster said to him: 'Congratulations, Larry, you've got your relief job.'

When Larry got to work he got out the Red Book of *Regulations for Train Signalling* and laid it open on the locker top to swot between trains. Now, during the day there had been single line working between Rattery and Brent, because one of the twin-bore tunnels at Marley had been closed for repairs. The work was complete and the engineering train was in the section between Ivybridge and Hemerdon, Cornwood being switched out. Larry had pulled off for the train and was talking to Jimmy Roberts at Ivybridge about his academic efforts, because Jimmy too was brushing-up since his annual rules and regulations inspection was in the offing. Jim asked Larry, 'What would you do if you were here and you had that down engineering train break away at Cornwood after dropping off the p-way men?'

No sooner had he said this than a voice broke into the conversation. 'This is the guard of the engineering train. We've broken away on starting at Cornwood after dropping the p-way chaps.'

As Cornwood box was closed and locked, Jim Roberts thought it was impossible that anyone could be speaking on the Cornwood circuit. 'You can catch some people,' said he to the guard, 'but you won't catch Jimmy Roberts.

Where are you speaking from?'

'I've had to break into the groundframe at Cornwood.'

By then the front part of the divided train was clanking slowly past Hemerdon box, to stop at the stop board to allow the (absent) guard to pin down brakes. Larry could see it was indeed incomplete and told Jim that they were not having their legs pulled.

Jim and Larry between them decided on the course of action to take, with the guard of the train listening on the phone at Cornwood. They agreed that the engine provided for the use of the pilotman during singleline working, which was still at Ivybridge, could be used to collect the broken-away wagons. Jim instructed the driver to pass Ivybridge starting signal at danger and to enter the section to Hemerdon, being prepared to stop and pick up the guard walking back from Cornwood, who would guide him to the rear of his train. The wagons would then be propelled — pushed in layman's terms — to the home signal at Hemerdon, where they would be met by the fireman, who would conduct the train safely to the front part. Two beats on the bell from Ivybridge, acknowledged by Hemerdon, authorised the movement to commence. When this was done Larry got on his motorbike and went down to the stop board to inform the driver of his loss and to tell him to send his fireman back to the home signal and there await the arrival of the rear end of his train.

An incident of a broken drawbar at Hemerdon also shows how matters were handled in steam and semaphore days. Larry was on nights and had put a goods train into the up loop to allow the Penzance-Paddington sleeping car train to pass. On giving 'Train out of section' to Plympton for the sleeper, he was 'asked clear' for the Millbay-Old Oak Common empty coaching stock train. He gave the road for it but it was running very early. Larry did not think it was right to delay a loaded goods train for an early-running train of empty stock and so, when the sleeper cleared Ivybridge, Larry got the road for the goods and pulled off out of the loop. With that the 'stock' was belled 'on line' off Plympton. It came up the 1 in 41 very briskly and it was plain from the music of the exhaust in the night that it was double-headed. The goods, of course, was still making its way to Ivybridge and Larry checked the 'stock' at the up home and up starting and brought it to a stand at the up advanced starting. When the goods cleared Ivybridge, he got the road for the 'stock', 2-2-1 on the bell, and pulled off but the train did not move. Then he saw two white lights coming back along the train towards the box. The fireman and guard came in to report that the drawbar of the leading vehicle, a very old parcels van, had been pulled out of the headstock. When the drawbar came out, the vacuum pipe between the van and the engine's tender was pulled apart and the whole train came sharply to a stand. The old van's vacuum pipe was the one torn, that on the engine's tender was all right. This old van had been in use as a stationary store at Millbay for years and was being taken for scrapping. Its handbrake did not work and it was running without a vacuum brake but with a through pipe.

The guard, Larry and the fireman conferred as to how to get out of the situation. The old van had to be put into the loop but it could not be pulled, only pushed. The third vehicle from the engine was astride the loop points and in any case the train could not move until the vacuum brake was released, which would have to be done by an engine at the rear of the train. Larry called for the banking engine out of Tavistock Junction Yard. It came to the rear of the train and coupled on. The train was split at the front between the second and third vans and the vacuum pipes put on their stops. The vehicle coupled behind the damaged van was, by great good fortune, not an ordinary carriage but another parcels van with an effective handbrake. This handbrake was pinned down. The banking engine eased the rest of the train backwards, drawing it clear of the points. Larry turned the points and the engines now pushed the damaged van with the well-braked parcels van on the Plymouth end of it, into the up loop. The engines could now rejoin their train and leave. The entire operation, from calling for the bank engine, had taken about 90 minutes.

Larry took up his relief signalman job in Plymouth No 2 District, in January 1953. His district was any box from Manamead, just east of Mutley Tunnel, Plymouth North Road, westwards to Treverrin, a break-section box between Lostwithiel and Par. Normally Plymouth No 2 reliefmen would only work the Plymouth local boxes to save the additional costs to the railway of lodging allowance and travelling time. Saltash reliefmen covered from St Budeaux to Menheniot and Liskeard men St Germans to Treverrin but there were times when Larry was sent to the furthest end of the district.

There were four Special Class boxes and two Class 1s in the Plymouth area. Promotion had been slow in the Plymouth District for years, even before the war, because of the influx of redundant signalmen from South Wales, and so there was no chance of vacancies in these top boxes; but as a reliefman Larry could have the satisfaction of being qualified to work them and actually to do so as the occasion arose. Now he had to visit a dozen signalboxes and learn the working at each and then be passed by the inspectors on the rules and regulations as they applied at each place.

The first box he went to learn was one of the smallest and certainly the quietest — Millbay Crossing — and the last was no bigger than Millbay Crossing but was fiendishly busy — Manamead. Truly, the exertions of a signalman cannot be judged from the length of the lever frame. Manamead sat just outside Mutley cutting and had six levers for distant, home and starting signals in each direction, and was simply a break-section box on the doubletrack bottleneck between Plymouth North Road East and Lipson Junction. The doubletrack section was in constant use with Western and Southern Region passenger and freight trains, light engine movements, empty stock and goods transfer trips. Half the down trains offered on to North Road East by Manamead were accepted under 2-2-2, 'Line clear to clearing point only', so the signalman at Manamead did not pull his stop signals until the train concerned had passed his distant signal at caution. Almost all the others were accepted by North Road East under the 'Warning arrangement', 3-5-5 on the

The interior of North Road East looking from the east end of the box, levers 6 to 185. Special Class Signalman Willie Werrin is at the centre with Bill Baldock next behind him. A goodly array of wooden-cased telephones adorns the walls above the standard GWR signalmen's lockers in cream and brown. Other antique GWR furniture, all built at Swindon, is on show, plus a magnificent iron stove. At the far end, what appears to be a wardrobe is the steel air raid shelter. This view was taken on 5 August 1941, with a good deal of bombing yet to come, and one wonders if the men drew lots as to who should use the shelter and how Willie Werrin would fit himself into it if he won the draw! *GWR/Larry Crosier Collection*

bell. The only time that North Road East gave full 'Line clear', allowing the Manamead signalman to pull his down distant signal, was on a summer Saturday when the 10.30am Paddington, the 'Cornish Riviera Express', was scheduled to run through North Road nonstop. From Lipson to Manamead was ⅞ mile and to North Road East ⅜ mile. In such very short, heavily occupied sections, bell ringing, lever pulling and train register keeping was a concentrated activity but there was an added complication — route codes. In the absence of train describing instruments, every category of train had its own descriptive bell code. WR express passenger trains were belled in the standard way, four beats, but a Southern express was 2-2-1-4. A WR local passenger train was the standard 3-1 but a Southern was 2-2-1-3. Railcars to Plympton were 3-1-3 and to Saltash 4-3-1-3. Passenger trains to Tavistock were 1-3 and railcars for Tavistock 3-1-3-1-3. Southern railmotors and light engines had many destinations and bell

Looking northeast from the main road bridge over the River Tiefy at Carmarthen station, as No 2217 waits patiently at the up inner homes for Carmarthen Crossing box, probably with a train from Aberystwyth. At the far end of the train is the down starting signal for Carmarthen Crossing, with the distant signal for Carmarthen Goods Yard beneath it. The scene dates from July 1962. *George M. Staddon/Colour-Rail*

codes to go with them. The standard code 2-3 indicated a light engine for Tavistock Junction Yard or the main line beyond. A 4-2-3 was a light engine to Cornwall, a 3-2-2-3 was one for Laira Old shed if given on the up line bell but for Millbay if given on the down line bell. An engine for Laira New shed via No 1 curve and 'the speedway' was a 5-2-3. There were many more, including for different types of goods trains. Signalmen working Lipson Junction and the two Plymouth North Road boxes also used these codes.

Millbay Crossing was a 14-lever box deep in Plymouth's heavily blitzed dockland. The line was doubletrack from the old Millbay station, over the road, falling at a 1 in 50 gradient to the Ocean Terminal of Millbay Docks. Millbay Crossing controlled gates across a road into the centre of Plymouth and had six freight trips a day to and from the docks, plus any Ocean Specials that might run. These Ocean Specials ran according to the arrival of the transatlantic liners and therefore had no set timetable. What they did have was a set of point to point timings from Millbay to Paddington so that, given the time they left Millbay Dock, signalmen knew when to expect them to pass and could clear the road for them accordingly. There were varied time allowances between places according to the weight of the train, the fastest schedule being 'A', the slowest 'E'. The boat train was 'wired' box to box as a 'Plym' with its schedule indicated by the code letter. The Millbay Station Platform Inspector was responsible for starting the boat trains. The first intimation Larry had of the boat train was when the inspector telephoned Millbay Crossing from Princes Pier saying, for example: 'Boxer: Millbay Dock to Paddington. Plym A. 10.10.' This would be perhaps 20 minutes before the specified departure time.

Larry would at once send the box to box message on, as received, and it would go on through the boxes, eastwards. The signalmen all the way to Paddington would then make sure that they arranged a path for the train, giving it precedence over just about every other train on the line. Plympton, Hemerdon and Totnes, for instance, responsible for pathing goods trains up the steep banks, would particularly want to know about the running of the Plym A.

A minute or two before the stated departure time, the Millbay inspector would telephone and ask for the road, with a cheerful 'Right away the boat train!' Larry would 'ask on', four bells, to Millbay signalbox. The signalman there was ordered by his special instructions to lower his 'From docks' home signal *before* he returned 'Line clear'. When the Millbay Crossing signalman saw that signal lowered and saw 'Line clear' showing in his instrument, he would close his gates across the road and peg to 'Line clear' his single-decker Spagnoletti instrument, in communication with a non-pegging instrument on the pier. In that instrument an asterisk symbol ('*') would appear to indicate that the train was cleared to leave. Larry would then pull off his home and inner home signals. He had then committed himself and could not reopen the gates until the boat train had passed or he was told that it had been temporarily cancelled.

There was a very memorable and unusual day one winter when, the Millbay inspector having got the road, the train did not materialise and traffic began to build up on both sides of the gates, tailing back into the town and disrupting traffic in the city centre. The police came and demanded that Larry open the gates but he could not, since the train was, according to the regulations, on its way. He tried ringing the inspector but got no reply; clearly he was outside, attending to whatever problem had befallen the train. Eventually the inspector phoned. 'Sorry, we've got vacuum trouble, we were busy and I never thought of telling you. Cancel the Plym A and I'll ring you for it later.' Signals could then be restored and the gates opened.

A few days later, Larry was on early turn in the box. The previous day there had been heavy rain and during the night a very hard frost. At 1pm it was still bitterly cold. Larry had the road set and the signals off for an empty coaching stock to come away from the dock.

There was a spring trap point on the up line on the Millbay side of the gates to protect the road traffic from a runaway from the station, further up the hill. This trap point normally lay open but could be closed by a lever in the signalbox. When the trap was open as an ordinary spring trap, this lever was reversed, ie pulled over the frame. In this position the interlocking allowed the up home signal levers to be reversed and the signal lowered. If the signalman wanted to close the trap point he had first to put the up home and inner home signals to 'Danger' and then push the trap point lever 'normal', back into the frame.

The empty coaching stock came up the incline, the engine slipping and skidding until its train was straddling the open catch point, creeping forward but always in danger of stopping and running back — and derailing at the trap. Larry put the home signals back to danger and tried to push the catch point lever back into the frame and thus close the trap. The lever would not move more than an inch and felt springy to push. Larry felt sure the rodding was frozen in its channelling below the road. He called the Signal & Telegraph lineman. The lineman arrived and decided it was a locking fault, not his field. Larry told him to disconnect the rodding from the lever, whereupon the lever moved freely — not a locking fault.

'What are we going to do then?' asked the lineman.

'I reckon the rodding is frozen in the ducting under the road,' said Larry. 'There's a north wind blowing so if you were to light a fire at the north end of the channel, the wind would blow the fire down through and melt the ice.'

'Good idea!' said the lineman enthusiastically. He lit the fire and the wind carried it into the duct very successfully. Perhaps the ducting was full of litter, perhaps it was boarded-in with wood under the cobbles, but at any event, flames and black smoke began to billow up out of the cobbled road. Motorists were now filled with alarm on top of impatience and got hurriedly out of their cars. The police arrived and took a dim view — indeed, the smoke was quite thick and little could be seen. They hurried to the box and took an even dimmer view — it was the same man on duty who had held up the city a few days previously. But by this time the fire had done its work. The rodding was free.

Under a rainbow after a summer storm, No 6843 *Poulton Grange*, fresh from Swindon Works, hurries a Bristol-Swindon stopping train past Thingley Junction's down outer home signal, 827yd from the box, in 1958. *P. M. Alexander/Colour-Rail*

No 7005 *Sir Edward Elgar* at Hereford, perhaps with the up 'Cathedrals', waits for the road from Hereford Station box up home signal. The right-hand arm applies to the up middle road. *P. M. Alexander/Colour-Rail*

Coombe Junction on 4 July 1959, with the No 1 signal lowered for the 5.17pm Looe to leave for Liskeard. The train was hauled by No 4559, bunker-first from Looe. It stopped by the small overbridge, uncoupled, went ahead into a spur and came back through spring-operated points to the signalbox and returned to its train, now chimney-first for the steep, circular climb to Liskeard. The other arm, No 2, when lowered, was for the Looe direction. Its brass lever plate had the splendid legend: '2 to Looe Starting'. A ringed arm signal, No 25, by the bridge gives access to the Moorswater branch.
Peter W. Gray

Having arrived at Falmouth with the 5.15pm Truro, No 5533 pushed its train back on the down line to the signalbox. It then ran across to the up main. While this was taking place, the guard placed the tail lamp on the rear of the train. The backing signal has been lowered for the engine to run round its train. When the engine gets onto the Truro end of its train, it will propel it back, over the crossover to the up main platform, which lies behind the photographer.
15 May 1959.
Michael Mensing

4. Liskeard, Largin and Looe

Of all the signalboxes Larry worked as a reliefman, the one he enjoyed most was St Germans. The village was a very close-knit place but this did not make them resentful of strangers and, in any case, Larry's mother was born at Tideford, a couple of miles away, and there were many relationships between the two villages. Larry had an uncle at St Germans. On the first day that Larry went to St Germans box to learn the job, Arthur Bennett was the signalman. 'Ever been to St Germans before?' asked Arthur.

'Oh yes, I got an uncle lives here — Jim Colwill.'

'Oh, I know Jim. And I knew your grandfather too. He was the village snob [cobbler, I hasten to add for those unfamiliar with the Cornish] and a bloody good snob he was. Now then,' continued Arthur, changing to an explanatory tone of voice, 'St Germans isn't like any other box you'll come across, so you'd better take note of what I say. This here is Alan's locker. This is Jack's in the middle — it's the only one with a lock and the key's hung up here. The radio's in there, and mine's at the end here. If the D.I.'s about you put the radio in Jack's and lock it. If anyone comes up to pay his National Deposit [a friendly society with local agents paid a commission on their collections] you sign his book, make a note of his name and put the note and the money in Jack's locker. If anyone comes up for cigarettes — they're in Jack's locker.'

The fags were in the British Automatic Company's slot machine on the station and the stationmaster was custodian of the packets of cigarettes for restocking the machine. The villagers living near the station bought from the machine and the money was collected by the stationmaster and paid into the station's account. When tax increases made it impossible to put the right money into the machine, the stationmaster cleared the machine and brought the old stock to the signalbox to be sold at the new price. The men then pocketed the difference. Alan collected the subscriptions for the Liskeard Branch of the NUR, and Jack collected for Saltash NUR, so besides smokers there were railwaymen coming into the box to pay their subs. Arthur Bennett concluded his briefing to Larry: 'Anyone comes in to order basic slag, take his name and leave it in my locker an' if anyone comes in and asks for a grave to be dug, don't worry, just take his name and address and put it in my locker, because I'm the sexton and I've never had a complaint from anyone I've dug a grave for.'

The St Germans stationmaster was 'Daddy' Parsons. Jack was due for late turn one afternoon but his wife came to the station to report him sick. 'Daddy' came to the box and rang the Plymouth District Inspector, Percy May. He began formally but was unable to keep it up for more than a few seconds. 'Good morning, sir. Is that you Mr May? Well, look here, Percy, Jack Medlin's gone home sick. What are you going to do about it, son?'

When Larry was relieving at St Germans the bus, train and ferry timetables made it difficult to get there in time on early turn and to get home at some reasonable hour off late turn. The result was that, if Larry was required for a 6am to 2pm shift, he was paid to lodge at St Germans the evening before but what he, and every other reliefman did, was to go down on the 6.10am Plymouth, getting to St Germans at 6.44am and the night shift man would hang on for him. But, to pay back the local men, the reliefman worked till three, when the late turn man came on, allowing Larry to catch the 12.00 noon Penzance at 3.15pm for Plymouth. A Plymouth reliefman, working nights at St Germans, relieved the late turn man at 9pm.

St Germans worked with Wearde towards Plymouth and Trerule, a six-lever, break-section box, towards Penzance. About 14 months after Larry did his first shift at Trerule, it was abolished and its down distant and down home signals were operated from St Germans, after 'Line clear' was obtained from Menheniot. Trerule thus became an 'IBS' or intermediate block section. One day when Larry was working St Germans, lightning struck the transformer processing mains current for the IBS. Every train had then to be stopped at St Germans box and be given a form with written authority to pass Trerule IBS home signal at danger. (This was a GWR regulation eventually dispensed with by British Railways.) This meant that heavy trains were restarting on a 1 in 78 gradient (which steepened after ¾mile to 1 in 68 for a further mile) and their firemen were unhappy at the extra coal this procedure consumed. The

Looe station, 25 July 1957. The fine GWR bracket signal is the down home signal. No 7 arm is lowered for No 4552 to pull its train onto the harbour line to run round, prior to returning to Coombe Junction and Liskeard.
K. R. Pirt

A view taken just over two years later, on 29 September 1959, shows No 4585 pulling out of the station to run round. It also illustrates that the bracket signal had been removed (in February 1959) in favour of a pair of ground discs, which can be seen by the leading coach bogie. In the background is the up starting signal which is common to both views.
Peter W. Gray

Looe, probably the smallest signalbox on the GWR or BR(WR). It housed eight levers, a diagram of tracks and a lamp repeater for the distant signal. The electric key token instrument was in the parcels office. 25 July 1957. *K. R. Pirt*

transformer was not repaired for several days, and a day or two after the incident Larry walked to Devonport station with a fireman friend of his, who was also going on duty. 'What are you working today, Jack?' asked Larry.

'We've got the 'Murphy' from North Road. Have they got Trerule IBS working yet?'

'No.'

'Well it's a bloody nuisance having to stop for that form, tears holes in the fire.'

'Well,' said Larry, 'I'm at St Germans today an' I'll tell you what I'll do. I'll make a loop of stiff wire and fix the form in it and hold it out, then you can pick it up without stopping, like the staff.'

The 'Murphy' was the 7.40am Newton Abbot to Penzance passenger train, nonstop from Saltash to Liskeard. It carried that nickname in remembrance of a Passenger Train Inspector who had retired some years earlier, whose main object in life was, it seemed, to chase any delay at all to that train before all others.

When the 'Murphy' came off Wearde, Larry 'asked clear' from Menheniot and checked the passenger at his home signal, lowered it and went to the platform with his wire hoop and official form. The 'County' on the 7.40 came up to the box giving it gunfire, Jack leaning over the side with arm outstretched. He snatched up the rude hoop and the train drummed past. They had lost two minutes on normal running time and saved about 10 minutes compared with the delay caused by stopping and restarting up the steep incline. Larry and Jack met up on the way to work the following morning. 'That was a proper job, yesterday' said Jack appreciatively.

55

'Well, you won't be doing it again, they've got the IBS working now.'

The following day an internal letter arrived in St Germans box for Larry: 'Two minutes delay at St Germans to the 7.40 Newton Abbot. Please explain.' How was Larry to tell them that he had saved the train *10* minutes by means of his very unofficial way of delivering an official form? Would he simply have to disguise it by confessing to tardiness in pulling-off instead?

Trerule box had six levers in a larger frame, because it had been intended to work the junction for the new line to Looe which the GWR had intended to build in the later 1930s. Arthur Bennett had worked there at times during the war and remembered how, during the nervous weeks of June and July 1940, when the threat of invasion hung in the air, he had been there on night shift and in the middle of the night his blood had frozen when he heard a furtive sort of metallic clinking noise and he wondered whether the Germans had landed. He waited with bated breath but the noise started and stopped and did not get any closer. The trains passed, the night wore on and as dawn broke he saw — not a field full of German soldiers but a cow, trailing a chain stapled to a wooden stake.

When Larry had shifts there, the box was open from 5.30am to 9.30pm. When on early turn he went by motorbike, caught the 4.15am Torpoint ferry and was in Trerule box by 4.55am. The first thing to do was to light the Tilley and then the fire, and then the fire in the 'packers' hut' and put their cast iron kettle on it, so that all was comfortable when they arrived for work about seven o'clock.

One morning Larry found a locomotive's storm-sheet suspension spring lying on the lineside. He drove a nail into the hut's wooden door on the inside, hung the spring on it and then a firebucket with a stick across it and an old macintosh around the bucket with the stick through the arms. He lit the fire, closed the door and retired to the signalbox to open up and await the gang with more than usual pleasure. Ron Wentworth was the first to appear. He leant his bike against the hut and opened the door. Of course, the clanking, springing 'man' jumped out at him, he sprang back in fright and Larry had a good laugh. About three weeks later Larry was working St Germans and the ganger came into the box. 'Here, we had a scare this morning. We was walking down towards the hut and saw the smoke out of the chimney and thought you was in the box. We opened the door and three blokes went tearing out past us an' ran off down the line. After your job the other week, that did give us a fright.' It turned out that the three were absconding inmates of a local borstal.

Menheniot box Larry did not like. It was not the lack of mains electricity but the fact that it was a dismal place, by the quarry, and the interior was dirty and ingrained with stone dust. It was 'a proper old dump'. The quarry rock face was some way from the line and blasting operations were usually outside the 110yd limit of safety from the line, but occasionally some blasting was carried out within 110yd of the line and then the quarry foreman came to the signalman to close the section. If no train was signalled and there was a suitable gap in the

train service, Larry 'blocked back', 2-4 on the bell and section indicators to 'Train on line', and then gave the foreman a red, metal disc marked: 'GWR. Permission to Blast. Menheniot.' The station porter was posted on the station gate to prevent anyone coming on to the premises and the dynamite was exploded. The quarry foreman then brought the disc back, confirmed that everything was in order and Larry would take off the block by sending 2-1 on the bell and dropping the 'Train on line' indications.

The signalman had a down goods loop but the entrance was 350yd from the box and around a sharp bend — 350yd was the extreme permitted limit for mechanical operation of facing points. The sharp bend and the lack of track circuiting prevented Larry from seeing when the train was inside the loop and clear of the main line, and he had to wait for confirmation from the guard. This delayed by a couple of minutes the giving of 'Train out of section' and 'Line clear' to St Germans for the following train. Larry always kept a collar on the loop incoming signal lever.

The down loop at Menheniot was also used to take up goods trains off the main to avoid delay to a following passenger train.

When Larry went to learn the job at Doublebois (pronounced Doubleboys) he caught the 6.50am from North Road to arrive at 7.30. He was met by the incumbent signalman, Jack Rowe, a dear old boy who always had a smile on his face. Jack introduced him to the job like this: 'Well, there's nothing here that will upset you after working at Plymouth. Down goods trains must stop at the stop board to pin down brakes. So long as the down goods is off Liskeard half an hour before the passenger's due to leave here, you'll be able to let the goods run to the loop at Lostwithiel — otherwise you'll have to put her in the down refuge.'

'Oh, all right then,' said Larry.

'Right, that's that settled then,' replied Jack. 'Now you've come I can go home to breakfast. I live at No 1 in the cottages up there behind the box. I'll see you later.' Off he went leaving Larry in charge.

Doublebois signalbox worked with Liskeard to the east and Largin to the west. The station was at the summit of a very steep climb in each direction between Liskeard and Lostwithiel and was in fact the highest point attained by the GWR main line in Cornwall. Coming from Liskeard the line climbed for about 2½ miles from the Moorswater Viaduct, rising at gradients varying from 1 in 58 to 1 in 75, peaked and fell for a short way and then rose again to Doublebois. From there the line followed the young River Fowey, downhill for seven miles at 1 in 70/90/120 all the way to Lostwithiel and crossing on the way several viaducts, including the two highest in Cornwall: Liskeard, 150ft high; Moorswater, 147ft; St Pinnock, 151ft and Largin, 130ft.

Doublebois was a run-of-the-mill place from an operating point of view — except that the up refuge was on the down side. Larry was working there one day when he had an up goods which did not have its running time to Liskeard up refuge in front of the 7.45 Penzance-Crewe express. He knew he would

No 6850 *Cleeve Grange*, a Plymouth Laira engine, arrives at the up main platform at Truro with the up 'Cornish Riviera' on 11 May 1959. On the far left is the down bay with its starting signal. The next track is the down main, then a track known as the up branch. The train is passing from Truro West box up branch to down main home, with a very unusual, centre-pivoted backing arm bracketed out to the right for the facing points to the up main. To the right is a conventional backing arm. The locomotive has one BR(W)-pattern headlamp with its door open — I wonder if the paraffin vessel and burner are still within. The other lamp is a GWR pattern; the difference is in the shape of the carrying handle. *Michael Mensing*

No 4552 arrives at Liskeard branch station on 25 July 1957. The signalbox is a McKenzie & Holland product. Because of the circular route from Coombe Junction, the signalman could look across the curve to see his distant signal. The lamp case of this signal had its tell-tale light in the side, to shine towards the signalbox. Also because of the curve, the Liskeard branch signalman saw the tail lamp of the train before the engine passed the signalbox. *K. R. Pirt*

No 4569 leaves Bodmin with the 12.38pm for Padstow on a glorious day for a ride along the beautiful estuary of the River Camel, in September 1960. The signalbox here dated from the opening of the line in 1887, and contained 26 levers. In the foreground a fine GWR post, carrying stop and 'S' shunt arms, stands guard over the line to Bodmin Road. *Peter W. Gray*

knock a couple of minutes out of the 7.40am Newton Abbot stopping train, the 'Murphy', since he would not be able to give Liskeard the road for it while he crossed the up goods over the down line to the up refuge, but that delay was less than the delay that would be caused to the up passenger by letting the goods run. He crossed the goods and delayed the 7.40 by two minutes but gave the up passenger a clear run.

Next day came the 'please explain' letter from the Passenger Train Office at Plymouth. Larry told them he had to refuge an up goods in the up refuge to avoid delay to an up passenger. Back came the reply: 'I fail to see how refuging an up train could have any effect on the running of a down train.' Larry wrote back and suggested the office-wallah should learn his district properly and heard no more. Signalmen were fairly autonomous people in those days.

Larry also worked Largin box, one of the most lonely signalboxes in Britain. The box was situated at 270 miles and 1 chain from Paddington (via Bristol) on the down side of the line, between Largin and West Largin Viaducts, being immediately to the west of the former. The box had nine levers, no electricity, no running water or lavatory, just a Tilley pressure lamp for light and a little stove to heat food and water, which was collected from a spring running out of the ground nearby. Although it was lonely and high amid forestry, it had three regular signalmen, among them Jack Frater. He was the secretary of Lostwithiel station St John's Ambulance team, and each year had to attend the annual 'do' for the St John Ambulance Awards at Plymouth, so he took two nights off, which is how Larry found himself working the place.

It was simply a break-section box on the fierce gradient up from Bodmin Road and required no 'learning'. Larry's first trip was in deep winter, at night. He took his bike on the train and got off at Doublebois. It was about 1¾ miles along the railway line to Largin box. There was no cycling path along the railway, so he cycled along the A38 to where a rough lane turned left, crossed the River Fowey on a stone bridge and climbed at 1 in 6 up the valley side to a stone arch under the railway line. Leaving his bike in a handy hut, he scrambled up the precipitous hillside to the line in the dark and walked across Largin Viaduct to the box. A full, freezing gale was blowing, making the walk across the viaduct, set so high above the valley, as scary as could be, as the wind screamed up the defile, howled through the arches and threatened to blow him over the flimsy railings which substituted for a solid, reassuring, parapet. The dim, yellow lights of Largin box at the far side of this howling abyss were as welcome as a searchlight.

Largin worked with Bodmin Road box, where the occasional goods train stopped to drop off or pick up traffic. At around 3.30am he had a goods occupying the section to Bodmin Road and another one approaching him from Doublebois. He would have to stop this second goods. At this moment the Tilley lamp began to splutter, as it was running out of paraffin. So with the hand lamp Larry went looking round the box, in the cupboards, for more paraffin and

the funnel by which to transfer it to the vessel of the lamp, and the bicycle pump with which to pressurise the vessel — and the clamp-on burner which, soaked in paraffin (they did not have the luxury of methylated spirit), heated the vaporising tube. Clattering about, he found the equipment in the end, and then busied himself with the lengthy relighting process. Meanwhile, the second goods train passed his down distant signal at caution. The footplate men, feeling sure that the Largin 'bobby' had gone to sleep, crept their train quietly downhill to the signalbox, with the home signal, red, just ahead. Seeing the box in darkness, the enginemen were convinced the signalman was asleep. With the noise of the wind and rain outside, Larry did not notice them arrive until the engine's silhouette slid quietly to a stand, just outside. He was not bothered — Bodmin Road still had the section occupied so they would have to wait — and got on with his Tilley lamp. But then there was a sudden sharp grinding noise — like one of the box windows being slid sideways. Larry whirled round, heart in his mouth, and there was the engine's fireman leaping into the box shouting gleefully, 'What's on then, Bobby? You got the doss on?'

'No I haven't. You haven't got the road because they're shunting at Bodmin Road. And it's dark in here because this old Tilley lamp ran out of paraffin and I'm trying to relight it.'

The next box west of Largin was Onslow Sidings, sited on the up side at 272 miles 70 chains, which was opened for a few hours on summer Saturdays and for the daily freight to pick up and set down wagons for the clay works there. It was classed as a porter-signalman's job. Larry worked there once or twice and found it very interesting. He travelled from Plymouth to Bodmin Road on the 12.50am Paddington-Penzance newspapers, getting off at Bodmin Road about 10 minutes to six. His first task was to act as shunter and marshal the wagons to form the Bodmin Road-Bodmin goods; these had been put off by main-line goods trains during the night. He then became the guard of the same train to Bodmin. After working as the guard on two passenger trains on the branch, he finally arrived back at Bodmin Road where he was relieved by a guard. He had a bite to eat and then walked 1½ miles to Onslow Sidings and opened the box to let the local goods train, worked by a Bodmin branch engine, in to shunt the sidings. The down distant signal was no less than 1,920yd from the box and there were two reverse curves in that distance but, Larry thankfully recalls, the distant was a lighter pull than many another on a shorter, straighter wire run.

The Liskeard-Looe branch was also part of Larry's itinerary and a very pleasant one indeed. The branch had a curious history and this was reflected in the peculiar layout at Liskeard. The Liskeard & Looe Railway Company (L&LR) had begun life in 1825 as the Liskeard & Looe Union Canal and had been converted to a standard gauge railway after an Act of 1858 — an Act, by the way, which did not permit the company to change its name. The railway joined end-on with the Liskeard & Caradon Railway (L&CR) coming south

Perranwell signalbox, with 21 levers, on the Truro-Falmouth line was opened in 1894. It superseded a pair of groundframes which worked the points and the up and down disc and crossbar home signals and semaphore distant signals. A kind of interlocking between home signals and points was achieved by simple 'wire and slide' detection. Until 1892 trains were regulated over the single track *without* a Train Staff, messages being sent using double-needle telegraph instruments supplied by the Electric Telegraph Co. These instruments were located in the station. This system was replaced by Webb-Thompson Electric Train Staff (ETS) in January 1892 and these were transferred to the signalbox in 1894. The ETS working to Penwithers Junction was replaced by Electric Train Token (ETT) in April 1961 and the other in 1962. The box closed in April 1966. This photographed dates from 20 May 1959. *Michael Mensing*

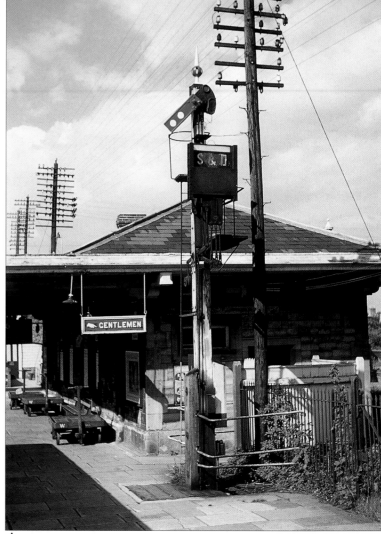

The Cambrian Railway bracket signal at Builth Wells, seen c1962. *Colour Rail*

The GWR backing signal on the down main platform at Highbridge, seen on 18 August 1963. The route indicator displays the legend 'S & D'; it could also display 'to shed', 'to up main', 'to up sidings' or 'to loop'. *Colour-Rail*

No 92235, after a long wait for a path 'through the Hole', drops out of the down goods loop towards the Severn Tunnel at Severn Tunnel East box, just out of shot. Note the second train waiting behind. Under the '9F's leading wheels and to the left is part of the scissors crossover between the up and down main lines, used for single-line working through the tunnel. December 1964. *B. Swain/Colour-Rail*

from mines up on the moor, and the latter company operated both lines — with horses until 1862. The junction was effected on the south side of the Moorswater Viaduct, 147ft below the Cornwall Railway (later GWR) main line. In July 1901 the L&LR opened its steeply graded link line from the valley floor at Coombe Junction to the GWR at Liskeard. Trains turned through about 290° and climbed 150ft in 2 miles. The L&LR was independent of the GWR and its trains were hauled by L&CR locomotives until August 1909 when the L&CR was leased by the GWR. The L&LR remained an independent company until 1 January 1923.

Because it was an entirely separate concern, the L&LR built its own, fully equipped station at right-angles to the GWR station at Liskeard. A siding connection to the GWR from the L&LR crossed the up main and trailed into the down main. This was controlled by Liskeard main-line box, giving shunting access to the branch. The signalbox, named Liskeard Branch by the GWR, was a Saxby & Farmer construction. When Larry was there the signalman acted as stationmaster, porter and shunter. The box was open from 6.10am to 10pm in two shifts and worked with Coombe Junction using the electric train token.

During the night, main-line goods trains would stop at Liskeard and reverse to the Looe branch to put off traffic for both the main line station and the branch. Up to 30 wagons might be waiting for the early turn branch signalman. Most of these would be for Liskeard main-line but there would be two or three for Moorswater and a couple for Looe. The Branch signalman assisted the Liskeard shunter, working with the branch '45xx' class engine, to sort the wagons into their three destinations. The branch traffic was positioned conveniently and then the engine took away the Liskeard main line traffic to run round it and push it down into the goods shed. While this was being done, the Branch signalman swept the branch station platforms, cleaned the lavatories, and then went to the box to operate the points and signals for the engine, which had come back from the main line and wanted to get on its coaches for the 7.25 departure.

Coombe Junction was something of a curiosity. Like Liskeard Branch box, it had a Saxby & Farmer, catch-handle locking frame until about 1958, when the worn-out frame was replaced with a WR standard pattern. This took away some of the flavour but the operating was still odd and interesting. The single line from Liskeard made a junction with the single line from Looe just south of the signalbox. The single track passed over a level crossing beside the signalbox and then forked, with one single line, classed as a 'long siding', going straight on, northwards, underneath the Moorswater Viaduct to Moorswater, the other turning right into the platform. At the viaduct end of the platform line, a spring point gave a run-round facility. The line from Moorswater had a trap point north of the viaduct to protect the spring point and any running-round movement that might be taking place.

A train arriving from Liskeard was signalled into the platform line. The fireman uncoupled his engine from the train at the far, viaduct, end of the platform line and the engine ran round its train, pushing through the spring point which then snapped back into its normal position. The electric token was handed off as the engine passed the box. It set back on to its coaches and then set off for Looe.

When the train arrived at Looe the signalman there gave 'Train out of section' and immediately 'asked clear' for it to return, even though it would not be leaving for half an hour or more. The Coombe Junction signalman replied to this with a full 'Line clear' or with the 'Warning acceptance', 3-5-5 on the bell, if he was expecting a train to come down from Liskeard or from the Moorswater direction.

There were one or two periods of about 10 minutes during the day when the signalman at 24-lever Coombe Junction was working at a higher rate than Old Oak Common East, which was the busiest box on the Western Region.

An example of this was when the 8.55am Liskeard-Looe cleared Looe at 9.25 and at once the Looe signalman 'asked clear' for it to return. The Coombe Junction man was expecting a light engine from Moorswater to Liskeard and, after that, the 9.55 Liskeard-Looe. These trains would be fouling the Looe line so Coombe Junction replied to 'Is line clear?' from Looe with 3-5-5. Five minutes later the Coombe Junction signalman would hear the engine from Moorswater whistling-up. He would then 'ask clear' to Liskeard and obtain a token, and pull off for the engine, whose driver collected the electric train token as he passed. 'Train out of section' was received from Liskeard at about 9.38 and at 9.45 Looe sent 'Train entering section' for the up passenger. At Liskeard Branch the engine from Moorswater was being coupled to coaches to form the 9.55 to Looe. At about 9.50 Liskeard Branch 'asked clear' for the 9.55 and Coombe Junction released the token instrument. At 9.55 came 'Train entering section'.

The Coombe Junction signalman set up the route to the platform line, the train ran past the box and handed off the token. The engine ran round its train. The signalman now lowered his signals for the train to go towards *Liskeard*. The train pulled out until the rear was clear of the platform/Moorswater siding points, the route was reset and the train set back on to the siding. By this time the 9.45 Looe had arrived at the home signal. The route was set for the platform and the signals lowered. The token was handed off as the engine passed. The signalman put it into the instrument, gave 'Train out of section' and at once 'asked clear' and removed the token for the 9.55 Liskeard. Once the Liskeard had gone, the engine on the Looe could run round its train, the signalman got out the token for the Liskeard line, set the road, and the train left. Peace and quiet then descended on the sunny valley but between 10.00 and 10.10am the Coombe Junction signalman had made 64 lever movements and operated the token instrument four times.

The signalman pulled off for the train but it was the guard's responsibility to start it. This is the 5.20pm Bristol-Severn Beach on 20 September 1955, with so many coaches to accommodate home-going workers that it cannot fit on to the platform at Patchway station. It is hauled by 2-6-2T No 6107; the reader might enjoy the mental contemplation of the sight and sound of this moderately sized locomotive ascending the 1 in 75 of Ashley Hill Bank with such a load. *R. C. Riley*

Only a lack of money prevented the GWR from installing more power-signalled, colour-light layouts. These GWR-designed, Siemens-built signals control the exit from Platform 7 at Bristol Temple Meads. The left-hand top head routes to the up relief line, with its 'calling-on' head below it; the right-hand routes to the up main. They are operated from Bristol Temple Meads East box — which contained 368 draw-slides to operate points and signals, and had 23 block bells. Proceeding nobly away from Platform 9 is No 5044 *Earl of Dunraven* with the 2.15pm Weston-super-Mare to Paddington on August Bank Holiday 1956.
Michael Mensing

No 5076 *Gladiator* with the 4.35pm Weston-super-Mare to Paddington, the 'Merchant Venturer', passing Bristol East Depot at 5.27 — if it left Bristol on time — on 19 September 1955.
R. C. Riley

Bristol East Depot No 2 signalbox was erected in 1894 and contained a frame of 69 levers. The cutting was formed when Bristol No 1 tunnel was opened out when space was needed for additional running lines and marshalling yard in connection with the opening of the Severn Tunnel in 1886. The GWR later changed the way it named its signalboxes, dropping the use of numbering before 1910. This box then became known as Bristol East Depot Main Line — the old Bristol East Depot No 1 became St Anne's Park. *GWR/Adrian Vaughan Collection*

Part of the block shelf in Parson Street Junction signalbox, Bristol, in 1974. A Tyer's train describer is nearest the camera, then the bell and GWR 1947 block instrument working with Malago Vale box on the up and down relief lines. The next train describer indicates a train for Temple Meads. Note the radically varying shapes of the signalling bells, designed to produce distinctly recognisable tones. *John Morris*

No 5086 *Viscount Horne* crackling past Old Oak Common East box on the down main line, with the 4.45pm Paddington-Worcester & Hereford express on 7 September 1957. The signalbox was opened in April 1927 with a frame of 160 levers. It was made redundant by automation and closed in October 1962. *R.C Riley*

Confronted with a sight like this, it would be easy to believe that the Western Region was the Great Western. The Old Oak Common Locomotive Yard signalman has set the road for the flyover and lowered his GWR-vintage engine line starting signal for No 5029 *Nunney Castle* to drift up to Paddington. The engine was booked to work the 2.15pm to Gloucester and the reason for its superb condition was that HRH Princess Margaret was travelling to Kemble (for Badminton House) in a GWR Ocean Saloon at the rear of the train. As late as 12 October 1957, the GWR spirit — and luxury — was still very much alive. *R. C. Riley*

69

The Siemens power frame of 224 levers installed in Birmingham Snow Hill South box in 1910. This controlled the double track to and from Moor Street through Snow Hill Tunnel and the tracks fanning out into the station. There were two island platforms and two through lines with stop signals and scissors crossings halfway. Within the tunnel there were two sidings, one of which connected to the Bank of England's vault, where gold was transferred from the railway bullion vans, which had doors on one side only. In the top right corner of the picture is the train describer working to and from Moor Street box. Below is the tapper to work the block signalling bell to Moor Street. Next is the permissive block instrument worked from North box, giving South box 'Line clear' and 'Train on line' on the down main platform. Permissive working, allowing more than one train at a time into a section, was permitted on the northern half of the down main platform, and the number of trains in that section was recorded by illuminating the white dots below the large circular face. Platform 1, the bottom line on the signalbox diagram, was worked under absolute block — only one train at a time — because of the restricted sighting due to extreme curvature. Next is the signalling bell for up main Platform 7. This is followed by three permissive block instruments by which South box gives permission for North box to admit trains to the southern half of the station. A colour-light down home signal, routeing three ways, was just inside the tunnel at the station end. To the rear of the signal was a wicked, 1 in 45, 'U'-shaped gradient within the 596yd tunnel. So that no train would ever stop at this signal, a special signalling routine was enforced at Birmingham South. A down goods or passenger train was 'asked' from Bordesley North to Moor Street. Moor Street did not accept it at once but 'asked' Birmingham South. The signalman there would not return 'Line clear' to Moor Street unless (a) the line on which the train was to run was clear to the starting signal at the middle of the platform or through line or to the signal at the north end of Platform 1 and (b) the home signal was cleared. If 'Line clear' was not returned, the train would be stopped at Bordesley North and when it did leave it would have space in which to accelerate to 'rush' the tunnel. Light engines could be stopped at the home signal. The working was doubly unique: the home signal was off *before* 'Line clear' was given and the down distant came off when the down starting signal was still at danger. The down distant signal miniature lever in Birmingham South box was used so frequently that, long before 1955, it was worn down to half its original diameter by constant use. *Peter Barlow/Adrian Vaughan Collection*

No 1459 and one rather beautiful GWR coach were deputising for a GWR diesel railcar on the 1pm Dudley on 6 June 1957. Having arrived at the up main platform at Birmingham Snow Hill, it had to run round its train via the central scissors crossover, coming back in the wrong direction on the up main, and is seen here setting back on to its coach at the north end of Platform 7/8. The engine is standing beneath a GWR backing signal, which a few moments before had been lowered for it to pass on the up main. A similar signal applies to shunting movements from the up platform. The latter is not signalled for passenger trains to leave in the wrong direction but Platform 11/12 obviously is. *Michael Mensing*

GWR wooden arm and post signals were the most handsome semaphores in Britain. Some GWR S&T inspectors liked them so much that they protected them against replacement by tubular steel masts. The Taunton inspector, with a district from Highbridge to Burlescombe, replaced almost none of his wooden posts in a 30-year reign lasting until 1961 but the Frome inspector of the same period replaced them whenever he could. This one is the up Plymouth line distant for Aller Junction, worked by No 1 lever, a 2,104yd pull for the signalman, until it was fitted with an electric motor. Seen on 11 July 1958. *Peter W. Gray*

Approaching Aller Junction on 14 September 1957 is No 7001 *Sir James Milne* with a train for Kingswear passing Aller's down relief to down branch home signal. The little arm routes to the goods loop at the foot of Dainton Bank; the right-hand arm signals from down relief to down main, the Plymouth line. The other group of three are the down main home, main to branch and main to goods loop homes. *Peter W. Gray*

The usual way of changing the staff or, in this case, the electric train token. The train is the 9.20am Newton Abbot to Moretonhampstead, hauled by No 5183 on 26 February 1959. *Peter W. Gray*

The glorious scene at Bovey on 19 February 1959, as No 4150 barks away, tokens changed, with the 10.45am Moretonhampstead-Newton Abbot. *Peter W. Gray*

Venn Cross, on the Barnstaple branch between Wiveliscombe and Morebath, was preceded, at the Wiveliscombe end of the layout, by a 246yd tunnel. To provide the drivers of down trains with a good view of the home signal through the tunnel, its spectacle was detached from the arm and mounted low on the post — and facing the opposite way to normal. This famous signal can be seen in the bottom right-hand corner, next to a 55mph speed restriction sign applying to up trains. At the up platform is No 6327 with the 10.50am Barnstaple Junction-Taunton, seen on 3 June 1963. *Peter W. Gray*

No 4700 works up speed on the brief downhill section past Aller Junction down goods loop before the ascent of Dainton Bank, the steepest main line gradient in England and Wales, in January 1962. *Peter W. Gray/Colour-Rail*

Aller Junction down main starting signal, off at a truly GWR angle of 60° for the passage of No 7022 *Hereford Castle* with a train of LMS coaches, as No 4561 comes by with an up goods. *Peter W. Gray/Colour-Rail*

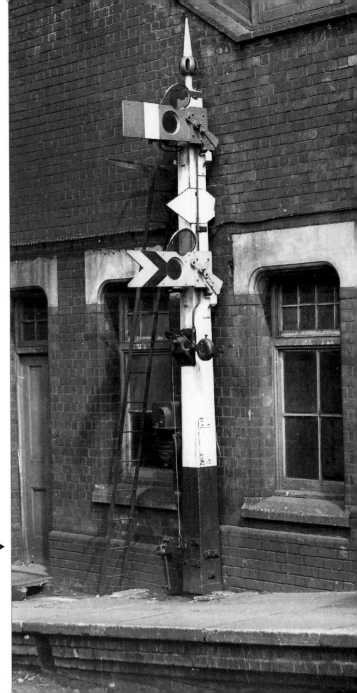

No 4125 on the up relief line passing Bordesley station and Bordesley South up relief line home and up relief to up main signals — the base of the signalbox is just visible below the bridge carrying the Midland main line. The distant signals belong to Small Heath North box and the 3ft arm leads to the up goods line to the right. 20 July 1961. *Michael Mensing*

Looking south from the bridge at Tyseley station over part of the splendid layout controlled by the 136-lever Tyseley South box. This is the junction for the North Warwick line to Stratford-upon-Avon and Cheltenham, Bristol and South Wales, opened throughout in 1906. No 7030 *Cranbrook Castle* is passing on the down main below GWR wooden post signals, Tyseley South's starting and Tyseley North's distant, with the 9.50am Paddington-Aberystwyth 'Cambrian Coast Express'. From the extreme left the tracks are: a headshunt siding; the up main; a trailing crossover; the down main; the up relief line; a trailing crossover; the signalbox; the down relief line; a set of facing points to the down goods running loop and a pair of sidings connecting with the North Warwick line. Against the wall of the box, a three-doll bracket signal routes: left-hand arm up relief to up main; up relief line; up relief to North Warwick line. 15 August 1959. *Michael Mensing*

Standing as smart and beautifully turned out as a Coldstream Guardsman, the down main home signal for Small Heath North with Bordesley South distant in 1960. The arms are of a special type, with the spectacle in the middle of the arm, normally used as duplicate arms when the main arm was placed on a very tall post; they are used here as the main arms due to restricted clearance. *Pat Garland*

Parson's Tunnel signalbox, with stupendous views over the sunny English Channel, could, perhaps, be regarded as a holiday home for signalmen. This box replaced an older wooden box when the line was doubled in 1906. It was mothballed out of service from 1909 to 1934 and in 1946 its frame was sent to Severn Tunnel East box. Parson's Tunnel box was restored to working order in 1947 with about eight levers. It was used for peak traffic periods in summer until 1964. No 6119 is passing the up main home on 14 July 1959. *R. C. Riley*

Almost the Great Western. No 4117 with a five-set suburban train and one main-line coach on the rear passes Parson's Tunnel box with an Exeter-Newton Abbot local. What a place to be a signalman! *R. C. Riley*

No 7304 arriving at Morebath with what looks like the school train from Taunton. The distant signal on the far right is on the Tiverton line and is worked from Lower Lodfin Crossing. *Peter W. Gray/Colour-Rail*

The signalman in Worcester Shrub Hill Junction has pulled off for 2-6-2T No 4175 on 1 June 1962. The engine is carrying 'B' headcode but, since it is running off the down middle road, my feeling is that this is a train of empty coaches. *R. C. Riley*

5. Flower Trains and Runaway Trains

Inspector May next asked Larry how he felt about going to learn Millbay Station box. Well — the bigger the better as far as Larry was concerned. Millbay had 115 levers but was rated only as a Class 2. In 1923 it was the fourth busiest signalbox on the GWR behind Ladbroke Bridge[1] (near Paddington) rated at 539 marks an hour, Old Oak Common West with 492 and Birmingham North power frame with 482: Millbay made 465 marks an hour[2].

In the Plymouth Blitz of April 1941, the adjacent goods shed was destroyed and so the station was closed to passenger traffic and turned over entirely to goods and to the remarshalling, cleaning and restocking of all main line passenger trains starting from or terminating at North Road. There was so much carriage shunting to do that a foreman shunter was in charge of the yard. The signalman worked at 'Special Class' rate during the day but the night shift was very quiet and the lack of lever movements during that shift reduced the overall 24-hour average, making the grand old box only a Class 2.

Passenger train formations had to be 'broken up' and remade and the yard foreman, having walked the trains and decided how he would rearrange the carriages, would phone Larry and from his memory would tell him all the shunting movements for the next three hours. Larry would write it all down in an impromptu code, on a slate using a piece of chalk. With the aid of the list, and watching from the window for hand signals, he could follow the shunters' operations, look out for their hand signals and move the points without any further communication being necessary. An inexpensive mode of proceeding, requiring only intelligent, interested workmen.

---

[1] This box was replaced with a new one named Ladbroke Grove in June 1927.
[2] To assess the volume of work handled by a signalman and thus determine his rate of pay, a totally detailed census of his actions was taken over a 24-hour period. A number of 'marks' were awarded for every conceivable action: for instance, pulling or pushing a lever, sending or receiving a bell code, each time a lever collar or a reminder flap on a block instrument was used, opening or closing level-crossing gates, using telephones or giving handsignals. The awarding of marks also took into account the daily average number of trains that had passed the box in the preceding 24 weekdays. Having reached a total of several thousand points, some very complicated arithmetic was undertaken, multiplying and dividing, adding 10% for this and 5% for that, until the 'average marks per hour' for the 24-hour period was obtained. From January 1951 the pay classification of signalboxes was on the following scale: Special Class B — 450 marks and over; Special Class A — 350-449; Class 1 — 280-349; Class 2 — 210-279; Class 3 — 150-224; Class 4 — 1-119.

84

Because Millbay station was a terminus, the down line was called 'arrival' and the up 'departure'. At the south end of the layout, near the station, was a series of facing connections: from the up dock line to the departure line, from departure to arrival and from arrival to the Harwell Street siding. The Harwell Street siding was accessible only to a northbound movement from the station end. The up dock line continued parallel to the departure line and merged with it at the north end of the layout. Until Larry's arrival at Millbay, if a trip from the docks wanted to get into Harwell Street, the signalman would let it up to the northernmost points, drop it back across the departure to the arrival line into the station and then forwards into the siding.

One day when Larry was on duty, the foreman's lengthy list of work ended with a 'trip' by the pilot engine and fish vans to Millbay Dock, returning with two parcels vans for Harwell Street. When the trip returned, Larry set the road direct to Harwell Street using the southernmost crossovers. Riding in one of the parcels vans were the shunters. The van was windowless. The train came to a stand and the men waited to feel their train reverse across the roads in the time-honoured way. They waited and waited and then someone suggested going to the box to wake Larry up. They opened the door to find themselves inside the siding. What a shock! It had never been done like that before.

A couple of days later, District Inspector Percy May went to Millbay Yard and asked Foreman Bill Fowler how Larry was getting on. Bill said he was happy with young Larry: 'We get there — but it's anybody's guess which way we go!' Mr May was so pleased with this that he told Larry to go and learn North Road East and West. Larry of course decided to learn West box with Cecil Wilcox who had taught him the job 10 years before.

North Road West, with its multitude of special bell codes, 60 levers, six platforms and its junction to Millbay, frequently used by trains of empty coaches, freight for the docks, light engines — and of course the Millbay-Paddington 'Ocean Specials' — was tremendously busy. Halfway through the second week of his learning, Mr May came to the box to see how Larry was progressing and was amazed to see that he was working with a confidence born of far longer experience than 10 days. 'How's he getting on, Cecil?' asked the inspector.

'He knows more about it than I do,' replied the signalman.

'In that case,' said Inspector May, turning to Larry, 'give me your certificate now and I want you here in the morning. Cecil's got to go for his medical tomorrow.' A reliefman wrote and signed his own certification of knowledge for each box he worked, just as an engine driver signed for his knowledge of the road he worked over. And that was how, by the time he was 24, Larry was in charge of Plymouth North Road West, a Special Class box, which he had learned as a schoolboy. The same happened when he went to learn the 185-lever North Road East.

The wonderful thing about being a reliefman — apart from the occasional high wages due to lodging turns — was the variety of the work, including having no work at all. If he was booked off over the weekend, on Monday morning Larry would telephone the office from the public call box near his house and ask for orders. If there was nothing at all required, Percy would say, 'All quiet, Larry — you'd better help Mother with the washing.' But planning any private life away from the railway was always risky, since he, and any reliefman, was always liable to be called out. The inspector would send the Devonport porter to Larry's house with a message to go to the public call box and phone in.

For example, Larry recalls a Saturday working at St Germans box. He had not been given any orders for the weekend and was looking forward to Saturday evening and Sunday off duty for once. At 2.50pm he was about to catch the 3.5 home to Plymouth when Percy May rang. 'Ah, I'm glad I've caught you. The Millbay man wants tonight off. It's urgent, can you cover it?' So Larry agreed and did 10pm to 6am at Millbay, a quiet turn, which was small consolation. He was still in bed on Sunday morning, sleeping off a long week of travelling and work, when the Devonport porter knocked on the door. Would he ring Percy May? Larry got up, dressed and went out to the phone box. 'The Menheniot down main outer advanced starting signal has been knocked over by an engineering train. Can you be at Menheniot for six this evening and work 12-hour nights until they've got a new signal put up?'

Larry went home and got a bag of food together and wheeled his push-bike out. He could have used his motor cycle but he knew that his friend reliefman Jimmy Foss was nights signalman at Menheniot and that he would use the 4.5pm railcar to Saltash and cycle from there. It was a beautiful afternoon and Larry thought it would be nice to cycle through the Cornish countryside with his friend.

On another occasion Larry was given the job of travelling 'on the cushions' of the 'Down Owl', 11.50pm Paddington to Penzance, to work back on the 12.5pm Penzance to Paddington flower train. This train stopped at all stations in Cornwall to pick up boxes of flowers. These had to be loaded into different vans and each van was marked with chalk outside to show its destination, and within each van again, chalked destinations showed where boxes had to be stacked, according to destination or transfer station. The boxes were loaded in hurriedly at each stop and sorted between stops.

In 1953 or '54, carriage cleaners were given the right to apply for the post of relief porter. Rather more experience was required for such a varied job as country station porter. Not so long after this alteration to the promotion procedures, the early turn porter at Doublebois needed the day off. His work involved the use of a shunting pole and also work in the booking office. The only relief porter available to Mr May was an ex-carriage cleaner who had

Par station c1925. A '517' class engine appears to have brought in the Newquay train and seems to have thrown a horsebox, taken from that train, towards the goods shed, and is now going into the headshunt. The next move may be to go around the train via the branch loop and the western crossover to the down main, to collect the main line coach on the down main and bring it back to the Newquay branch train.
Adrian Vaughan Collection

never used a shunting pole or worked in a booking office. So Mr May asked Larry to go down to Doublebois and cover for the porter.

The stationmaster was Bob Hocking. He had been signalman at Laira Junction when Larry was a lad telegraphist in Tavistock Junction box. Larry watched him deal with a passenger wanting a return to Liskeard and then Bob told Larry to deal with the next. A very trim, elderly lady bent down in front of the glass window and surprised Larry doubly by speaking in a Scots accent and asking for a first class return to Elgin. Doublebois ticket racks held tickets mainly for local places and some of the major Western Region destinations. There was no ticket for Elgin — neither was the fare written into the Fare Book. So Bob made some phone enquiries and ascertained the price of such a ticket from Liskeard and added the price of a return from Doublebois to Liskeard. Larry wrote out the blank card ticket and the lady handed over the fare — with that one ticket he took more than Doublebois normally took in a month.

Variety also meant working in two entirely different signalboxes in 24 hours. On a couple of occasions in high summer he worked North Road West all week and was posted to Looe on the Saturday. Here, the electric train token signalling instrument was in the parcels office because the signalman was in charge of the

No 4083 *Abbotsbury Castle* stands at Par's No 54 signal, up main starting, with the 1.30pm Penzance-Birmingham 'Perpots', on the occasion when Richard Riley travelled on the footplate on 9 April 1960. *R. C. Riley*

No 5198 climbs the 1 in 57 out of Par with a down stopping train formed entirely of GWR coaches in June 1960. Par's down main advanced starting signal is cleared, with Par Harbour box's distant off below. *K. R. Pirt*

The Par signalman, Roy Stockman, 'asks clear' to Lostwithiel after receiving 'Train entering section' from St Austell. There are three GWR 1947-pattern block instruments. That on the right communicates with St Austell; its needle can be seen at 'Train on line'. The portion of the diagram visible shows, from top left: the down goods loop, up and down main, the eastern crossover, connection to the branch platform and the branch loop. 22 June 1975. *Adrian Vaughan*

office. During the week the station was relatively quiet and the signalman could cover both jobs, walking from the parcels office to the signal levers at the end of the platform; but not on summer Saturdays.

When the first Saturday train arrived at Looe with hundreds of people from London and Birmingham, they all wanted to deposit their luggage at the cloakroom while they went into the town to find accommodation; even if they had accommodation, they were unable to get into the B&B before 11am. Every person had to pay five (old) pence and have a ticket written out. On these days, the fireman of the branch train handed the electric train token into the office and then operated the ground frame levers himself. When passengers' luggage was dealt with, there were mountains of outgoing luggage to be attended to, or else piles and piles of parcels to or from the town. The porter weighed them, called out the weight and consignee, and Larry entered the details on to the lorry delivery sheets or into the ledgers and then stuck the labels on them. The only breaks they would have on a summer Saturday were when a train token had to be put into or taken out of the instrument. And every train brought new crowds of people. North Road West was a doddle after Looe.

In January 1956 Larry was successful in applying for the post of Class 1 Rest Day Reliefman at St Blazey. None of the many more senior men had thought of applying and thus Larry was in a very senior position when he finally passed the rules and box knowledge examinations. The job gave him the opportunity to learn and extend his knowledge of the signalboxes west of Lostwithiel: to Treverrin, Par, the boxes on the Fowey branch north and south of the main line at Par — St Blazey Junction, St Blazey Bridge Crossing and Par Bridge Crossing — and continuing west on the main line to St Austell.

At Par he met for the first time the GWR 1947-pattern double-line block instruments. The box had been modified in preparation for the abolition of Treverrin and its replacement with power-operated signals worked from Par and Lostwithiel. Facing an examination on the rules from an unknown inspector, Larry wanted to know, 'What's the 'Old Man' like on the Rules?'

'Oh, not so bad,' said the Par signalman reassuringly. Larry was learning St Austell box when the inspector, Mr Edmonds, rang him and asked if he was ready to take his exam. 'Whenever it suits you,' said Larry.

'Come on up here to Par on the next train then,' replied the inspector.

Mr Edmonds met him off the train. It was a beautiful sunny day so he suggested they went and sat in a set of coaches standing on the branch siding. The questions began and Larry never had such a gruelling time. They went through the regulations and the Black Rule Book. And this was the man who was fairly easy on the rules! After several hours the inspector was satisfied. 'Have you got any questions for me?' he asked.

'Yes,' said Larry. 'I was told you were not too bad on the rules but that's the roughest time I've ever had on the rules.'

Mr Edmonds gave him a wry smile. 'Well,' he replied, 'I was given to understand you were very keen on them so I thought I'd take the opportunity to brush up on my own knowledge.'

Par was a busy junction and had a particular 'pathing' problem: the 11.5am Par-Penzance passenger, which only ran in the peak summer months, was always late leaving Par. This was because the footplatemen who worked it came up from Penzance on the 5.50am goods, which was always late. They were relieved at Par and walked round to St Blazey shed, where they took over their engine for the 11.5 passenger. They then came light engine to Par, and set back on to their coaches in the Chapel Siding at the west end of the layout. It would then be necessary to pull the stock out of the siding to the up main, run round, propel the carriages to the eastern crossover and cross to the down main platform. These manoeuvres took place within the clearing point and prevented the Par signalman from giving 'Line clear' for the 9.30am Falmouth-Paddington express. So the stock of the 11.5 Par remained inside the Chapel Siding. The 9.45am Newquay ran into the up branch platform at 10.40am. The engine was uncoupled and ran back to St Blazey shed through the branch loop. The Falmouth arrived at 10.43am. The engine off the Falmouth had to collect the Newquay coaches off the branch platform and set them back on to its train. Eight minutes was allowed for the shunting, so the Falmouth would leave late even if it arrived on time. Only when the Falmouth had gone could the empty stock for the 11.5 Par begin its manoeuvres.

Fred Lambton, the Par shunter, told Larry that no-one had been able to solve this shunting problem. This was the sort of challenge Larry enjoyed. The answer was to do the job the opposite way round — and for the men on the 11.5 to look sharp. As soon as they were on to their coaches they were to whistle-up. They would come out on to the up main and sprint smartly through the station, to the eastern crossover beyond the up main starting signal. There, they were beyond the clearing point of the up main home signal. Larry could give 'Line clear' for the Falmouth whenever it was required. Meanwhile he could reverse his eastern crossover for the empty stock to back across to the down platform and have an empty branch platform for the 9.45 Newquay. The 11.5 Par engine was by then uncoupled and could dash back through the crossover to the up main as the Falmouth was arriving. The engine off the Newquay went to shed and the 11.5 engine could follow along the branch loop, to the down main through the western ladder crossing. The Falmouth engine was by then setting back on to the Newquay coaches, while the 11.5 Par engine was setting on to its train in the down platform. Phew! It was 'playing trains' with a vengeance — and the best of it was that the 11.5 got away on time every day in the week that Larry worked Par. It caused a great stir at the Passenger Train Control and Larry received a congratulatory visit from Passenger Train Inspector Bob Hocking.

Nothing could be a greater contrast with Par than utterly remote Treverrin, which Larry worked on several occasions. A timber, six-lever, break-section box, without water or electricity on a 3-mile gradient from Lostwithiel to Treverrin Tunnel, it stood about 200yd east of the Tunnel. The box had to be opened at 11am. He came by train from Plymouth to Lostwithiel, arriving at 10.5 and then set out to walk 1¾miles along the trackside to the box. A friendly engine driver on a light engine stopped and asked him if he wanted a lift but the day was sunny and peaceful and it was a pleasure to be out, so he cheerfully refused the offer. The driver blasted away up the hill and Larry kept walking. When Treverrin box came in sight, Larry saw that the engine had set the lineside grass on fire close to the box. Larry hurried on but by the time he reached the scene, the fire had caught the wooden planking at ground level and was burning in the locking room. Luckily the rainwater butt was full and Larry filled a firebucket from this to fight the fire. The flames did not give up easily and the water butt was getting alarmingly empty by the time he had put the fire out — then he saw that a location box opposite the box was ablaze. This carried the connection for the block telegraph instruments and telephones but luckily it was not a large item and, scraping the bottom of the barrel, he extinguished that conflagration also. Sweating and sooty he went upstairs, switched the box in, tested everything and found all in order. Then he phoned Par and asked for the Signal & Telegraph lineman to attend to see what damage had been done in the location box fire. The lineman trudged up the hill an hour later. 'Oh, *that* location cupboard!' he laughed. 'You needn't have bothered — that was taken out of use a couple of weeks ago, it doesn't do anything.'

But the damage to the signalbox was so great that, even though it had only a few weeks of life left before being replaced by electric signals, the S&T carpenters had to come and make it structurally safe.

There were occasions when Larry was booked to work early turn Coombe Junction Monday to Friday and then open Treverrin for 3.30am on Saturday morning. On Friday he would go home, rest, pack Saturday's food and leave Friday evening for Lostwithiel, walk to the box and sleep there overnight, to be ready for opening the following morning.

Seventeen months after Larry became a Class 1 rest day reliefman at St Blazey, a Class 1 general purpose relief job came up at Plymouth North Road. He applied and, as the most senior man, got the job. He had a good send-off from St Blazey, which probably means a lot of beer flowed one evening. While he had been working in Cornwall, the west end of Plymouth North Road station had been remodelled in preparation for automation and the 60 levers in West box now had to do the work of a frame of more than 80 levers. This was achieved by making one ground signal show 'proceed' for any one of several routes, instead of having separate signals for each route. This was a potentially lethal arrangement, putting a great deal of extra responsibility on the signalman to set up routes carefully. Larry relearned this newly relocked lever frame and was passed for duty in November 1957. He worked the big North Road boxes for six months until, in April 1958, a vacancy arose for a Special Class signalman at Laira Junction. Larry applied for it and got it, due in part to his

seniority but also because many more senior Plymouth signalmen thought that the Laira job was spoiled by 'too many arguments with locomen'. The signalman here controlled movements on and off the engine shed.

For Larry, Laira Junction box was as near paradise as a living, breathing human being could get. A glance at the picture of the layout it controlled gives an impression of the complications involved but not of the enormous human interest of the place. Apart from the new 'Warship' diesels, Nos D600-4, the entire depot was dedicated to steam, from 'Kings' and 'Castles' to the humble '1400' class tanks. Besides this it was the practice for enginemen waiting to relieve goods trains to wait in the signalbox and Larry spent many hours a day working this splendid layout while listening to the reminiscences of enginemen from Laira, Penzance, Newton Abbot and further afield, many of them old enough to recall the pre-1914 Great Western. The railway ran not only on coal, sweat and swearing but also on tea, gossip and folklore.

Laira Junction was virtually at sea level beside the River Plym and the sea fogs and river mists were exacerbated by the smoke from the steam engine Running & Maintenance Depot. The allocation was 104 locomotives in 1947, so the place was a gritty, black, smoky, ashy hive of industry as the engines went through their servicing and came on and off the shed through Laira Junction. A signalman working a far-flung layout in darkness needed to pay attention with ears as well as eyes, listening for whistles requesting movements, attracting attention, as well as watching to see when movements had cleared the points. In fog this became a nightmare — by no means all the lines were track circuited and the engines' whistles were all a signalman had for a guide but they were very treacherous in fog. There was also the tremendous difficulty of spotting a train's tail lamp, which had to be seen before the signalman could give 'Train out of section' and accept the next one.

One night when visibility was nil, Larry heard an engine whistling at the up main home signal, 74yd west of the box. Larry had not accepted any train or engine from Lipson Junction, so he sent his fogman — who was employed to go out on to the line, watch for tail lamps and report back — to go to the up home. He also telephoned Lipson Junction but was told no up train had passed. The fogman came back and reported the line clear but still the engine whistled at the up home. Exasperated, Larry told the fogman to go and find the engine and not come back until he had. He found the yard pilot calling from the yard exit signal, wanting to go to shed. The yard exit signal was 219yd away and on a markedly different bearing from the box.

A rare sight indeed. Gloriously eccentric GWR signals sited on the remote route from Chacewater to Newquay at Tolcarn Junction, Newquay and photographed from the 4.25pm Truro-Newquay via Perranporth on 29 August 1959. The 3ft arm on the miniature bracket would signal goods trains only around the chord line linking this route to the Newquay-Par line. Tolcarn signalbox had 52 levers and controlled this triangular junction just outside the Newquay terminus. *Peter W. Gray*

The gantry at the east end of Newton Abbot station. The stop signals are worked from Newton Abbot east signalbox; the distant signals belong to Hackney Yard box. From left to right, the signals read: up through line to Moretonhampstead line home; up through line home; up main to siding; up main to Moretonhampstead home; up main home; up relief to Moretonhampstead home; up relief home; up relief to engine spur.
Les Elsey/Colour-Rail

St Blazey Junction looking north. The nearest signal has a 3ft arm for the Fowey line and a 4ft arm routing to Par, with Par's up branch distant fixed at 'Caution' below. 22 June 1975. *Adrian Vaughan*

On a very clear, frosty, bitterly cold night, Larry had both his cast iron stoves burning and by four o'clock the box was so hot he had opened one of the windows. The Tavistock Junction signalman 'asked clear' for the 9.50pm Paddington express about 4.10am, Larry gave the road and then got the road from Lipson Junction and pulled off. A few minutes later came through the night the booming sound of the GWR brake whistle — a runaway was in progress. Larry's booking boy, Mike Windell, had his head in the book of signalling regulations — for he had just been appointed to the eight-lever Woodley Bridge box in Sonning Cutting — and had not reacted to the emergency. Larry asked him if he had heard the noise and did he know what it portended — it was probably a freight train coming down Hemerdon Bank after the 9.50 Paddington, with insufficient brakes pinned down, so that the weight of the train had overpowered the brakes. With that, Tavistock Junction sent 'Train entering section', followed by 4-5-5, 'Train running away on right line'. The 9.50 Paddington was 'away'! Larry rang Jack Brokenshire at Tavistock Junction and was told that the passenger had gone through at what seemed like 90mph — the limit was 45. On the curve at Laira Junction the limit was 40. Larry could see the headlights of the train shaking violently as the engine came careering round Crabtree curve. The way it was travelling it could come off the curve and come straight through the box. Larry yelled at his booking boy to leave the box and, weighing the 'bolt from the blue' situation up in a few seconds, as all signalmen must, Larry reasoned that there was a 1 in 67 gradient up from Laira to North Road, the enginemen must be doing their best to stop and the steep rise would bring them to a stand. He sent the 4-5-5 on to Lipson Junction and followed Mike Windell as quickly as possible down the stairs, along the path and up the 30 steps of the nearby road bridge. The train roared past and in the dark Larry could see the brake blocks on engine and tender, white hot and ringed with sparks like Catherine-wheel fireworks, but the train's brakes were not even applied. The brakes on a locomotive are relatively weak; braking is designed to be done mainly by the carriages. With what brakes they had, the footplatemen brought their train to a stand outside Mutley Tunnel.

What had happened was that, in the bitter cold, condensed steam, as water, had collected in the bight of the brake hose between the tender and first coach and frozen, so that atmospheric pressure admitted by the driver's brake valve could not travel through to the carriage brake cylinders. The driver had called in vain with the brake whistle for the guard to put the brake on from his van, and it is easy to imagine the intense feelings on the footplate when the guard did not respond. Doubtless the latter kept well clear of the former for a while but sooner or later they would be rostered together again.

A chance in a million caused a derailment at Laira one evening. The 2pm Penzance-Paddington perishables hauled by No 5015 *Kingswear Castle* and formed of eight-wheeled vans passed the box. There was a loud crash and

Larry could see that two of the vans were off the road, jumping over the Tramway crossing. He threw the signals to danger and sent 'Obstruction danger', six beats, to Lipson and Tavistock Junctions. Larry sent a shunter to the ganger Nobby Penfound's home and phoned Control to inform them of the derailment and the need for cranes and a trainload of new track. The Laira yard master was at the cinema and the film was overprinted with a slide asking 'Mr William Bennett to report to Laira immediately'. The signalbox filled up with shunters, drivers and guards, all curious to know what had happened. After a while came the clanging of bells, and a fleet of police cars, fire engines and ambulances appeared on the bridge. Someone thought a passenger train was derailed and had called the emergency services. Larry was glad to be able to tell them all to leave. No injuries of any kind. Nobby Penfound was quickly on the scene and soon found the cause of the derailment. A spring hanger bolt on the tender of No 5015 had broken and fallen — upright — into the gap between the running rail and checkrail of a set of points. The following pair of bogies had been derailed by it but had bent it over, so the others rode it. The up main was closed for 24 hours.

By the end of 1965 steam was finished on the Western Region, and Plymouth Panel was due to take over the working of the mechanical signalling from Totnes to Penzance. Larry was a Special Class signalman but Plymouth had lots of signalmen in this grade with far more seniority than he. An inspector's job, with nothing to do with signalling, was advertised in Reading. He got it and left Laira Junction in 1967.

He and four other signalling enthusiasts, Dave Collins, Dave Wittamore, George Pryer and John Morris, formed the Signalling Record Society. Larry is proud to have been a GWR employee and steam age British Railways signalman — and to have done so much to ensure that the record has been preserved for the 21st century.

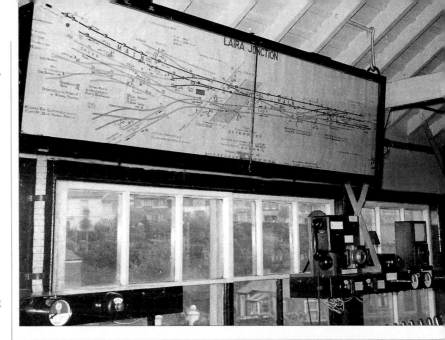

The Laira Junction signalbox diagram. This was taken in 1961, just after Plymouth Panel Control Centre had opened and was working with Laira Junction. Laira Junction's down main starting signal No 111 and Laira No 1 signal, up main distant, were three-aspect colour lights released by Laira Junction and Plymouth Panel, but the aspect they showed, on being released, depended on the occupation of the track circuited lines ahead. *Larry Crosier*

Laira Junction signalbox interior, with the gate wheel which once worked the crossing gates at each end of the level crossing of the tramway over the main line. *Larry Crosier*

Thorverton signalbox on the Exe Valley branch on 12 March 1960. Prominent instruments on the left are the control for the ganger's occupation key and the electric key token. Outside is the 3.25pm Exeter to Dulverton, hauled by No 1468.
Peter W. Gray

No 1470 shunting at Churston on 11 March 1960. It has brought a mixed train in from Brixham, pushing the auto-coach and towing two goods wagons and a brake van. Once the passengers had detrained, the shunter used his pole to uncouple the goods trucks, the signalman set the road and No 1470 shunted vigorously towards the sidings. The free-wheeling wagons have just disappeared out of shot to the right and the signalman has pulled off for the train to re-enter the station. *Peter W. Gray*

The end of a long day's photography as one red tail lamp wanders off into a symphony of red signal lamps at Bristol Temple Meads East on 13 August 1960. *Peter W. Gray*

Index of Locations Illustrated